Just Wondering, Jesus

Tom Ehrich

Just Wondering, Jesus

100 Questions People Want to Ask

morehouse

HARRISBURG • LONDON

Morehouse Publishing, P.O. Box 1321, Harrisburg, PA 17105

Morehouse Publishing, The Tower Building, 11 York Road, London SE1 7NX

Morehouse Publishing is a Continuum imprint.

COVER ART courtesy of Kwame Zikomo/Superstock
COVER DESIGN by Corey Kent

Library of Congress Cataloging-in-Publication Data

Ehrich, Thomas L.
  Just wondering, Jesus : 100 questions people want to ask / Tom Ehrich.
    p. cm.
  ISBN 0-8192-2146-5 (pbk.)
  1. Theology, Doctrinal—Popular works. 2. Christianity—Miscellanea. 3. Christian life—Miscellanea. I. Title.
  BT77.E44 2005
  242—dc22
                                    2004021671

Printed in the United States of America

05 06 07 08 09   10 9 8 7 6 5 4 3 2 1

Contents

Introduction

On a Monday in October, I asked a question. The answer changed everything for me.

Sitting in a hotel in Dallas, Texas, I began my daily discipline of writing a meditation on the coming Sunday's gospel reading. I send these out by e-mail to several thousand interested readers. My intention in "On a Journey" is to look for God in daily life. I have no axes to grind, no doctrine or cause I am trying to promote. I expect to be surprised and try to be open to new ideas and connections.

Using the hotel's Gideon Bible, I turned to Mark 10:46–52, the story of Blind Bartimaeus.

I reflected on the "street-level" experience of working a booth at a trade show and gathering with weary colleagues for dinner in Dallas's interesting West End. "Here we sit and talk," I wrote, "enjoying life at the only level where life can be enjoyed, the level of thoughts turned into words, listening and speaking, leaning forward to make a point, sitting back to savor stray glimpses of other lives at street level."

"Let's imagine," I continued, "that we could encounter God at this level. Not grand theology, not doctrines, not eternal truths, not tomes of analysis and argument, but street level. Or as in the case of blind Bartimaeus, the 'roadside.' If we could hear God passing by here, and if we dared raise our voice to God, and if we had any assurance, no matter what officious disciples say, that God would listen, what would we ask of God? Not, what ought we to ask? Not, what does the church tell us to ask? But what question would we actually lay before the Lord of life?"

I asked readers to send me their questions. I promised to spend the daily meditations between Advent and Easter trying to answer. I had no idea if anyone would respond. I pressed the send button shortly before returning to my consulting firm's booth at the trade show.

Responses came almost immediately. Two dozen came the first day, some within minutes of reading my inquiry, as if a question had been simmering, just waiting for an opportunity to burst forth. Seven dozen came the second day, and on it went, until I had received some 400 "Questions from the Roadside."

Initially, I just let the questions wash over me, like waves at the beach. Later I would categorize and analyze them. But for now I just tasted their salt, felt their intensity, and found myself being turned this way and that. I was overwhelmed and humbled. This was a larger sea than I ever knew existed.

The questions were so basic, so down to earth. They were like the request made by Bartimaeus, when he said, "Help me to see." The first to arrive was this: "Lord, what do you ask of your church?" "Why do children suffer?" was another. "Lord, am I on the right path?" "My Lord, please send me someone to love and to love me back." "Help me to break out of compulsion." "What and where is heaven?" "Will I ever be married with a family of my own one day?" "Why did you let my wife have the car accident that killed her?"

Hardly anyone asked about the controversies of the church. No one mentioned the gay bishop of New Hampshire, or the inerrancy of Scripture, or who controls Southeastern Seminary, or celibacy among clergy, or liturgical change, or laws concerning marriage, or separation of church and state. Given an opening to speak from their hearts, they asked about life, about God, about meaning, about eternity. They voiced despair and sadness, some caused by life's normal disappointments, some caused by religion itself. They voiced yearnings, many yearnings, and yet none of those yearnings was for money, career success, better sex, flatter stomachs, more successful children, faster cars, larger televisions, or anything sold by Wal-Mart or the Gap, or by the Republican or Democratic parties. Their yearnings were for healthier partnerships, clarity of purpose in changing times, love, hope, self-confidence, freedom.

Once I started answering the questions in late November, even more questions arrived. They continue to this day. Meanwhile, I tested a growing conviction. In February, I facilitated a leadership retreat for a congregation in Louisville. Rather than the usual teachings on leadership methods, short-term decision-making and long-range planning, I told these dozen lay leaders the story of "Questions from the Roadside." I asked for their questions. At worship the next morning, a lay leader simply read his colleagues' questions as the prayers of the people. He was weeping by the end. For their questions were just as basic, just as filled with yearnings and sadness, just as beseeching of a good and gracious God.

Again, I was humbled and startled. I would like to say that I had seen all of this coming. But I hadn't. That, in turn, raised the question: Do church leaders know what questions their people are asking? If they did know, would they continue doing what they are doing?

If the preacher knew that people were grappling with loneliness, grief, or doubts about purpose, would he still walk politely and intellectually through an exegesis of Scripture, offering precise translations of Greek words and clever anecdotes? If the pastor knew what was happening in people's homes, would she still spend her days attending meetings? If judicatory officials knew the despair their clergy are feeling, would they still offer carefully phrased position papers on official issues? If lay councils could hear questions from fellow parishioners, would they still lead in the usual way? If the small core group that tends to shape congregational life could hear questions being asked by the other ninety percent, would they still see the congregation as a projection of their own interests and personalities? If we knew each other's questions, would we behave differently in worship and church life?

This book offers 100 questions from the roadside and my answers to them. These aren't the only questions being asked. Nor are these the only answers. But I hope you will find authenticity in these pages. I hope you will be emboldened to ask your questions and to seek answers. I think religion has become too formulaic, as if there were only certain questions worth asking and only certain answers to be found. Life is too chaotic for such rigidity, and God too restless for such right opinion.

I will warn you, however, that once you start addressing real questions, it is difficult to fit back into the formulas. I grew up in the Episcopal Church and took its standard questions seriously throughout my youth and on into eighteen years of parish ministry. I served wonderful congregations in Indiana, Missouri, and North Carolina. I attended church conferences and national conventions and joined the usual debates. In my parish leadership, I thought of myself as a change agent, but I realize now that I rarely strayed too far outside the box. In the decade since moving on to writing, publishing, and business consulting, I have allowed myself more freedom just to see what there is to see, to ask whatever questions seem pertinent, and to read the gospels with no ecclesiastical constraints. As a result, I am ruined forever. Life inside the box holds no appeal. I yearn to belong, to be part of a vibrant Christian community, but not at the expense of putting aside real questions and rejoining sterile bickering over safe issues.

This book, then, is my attempt to serve. Stories are from my life, questions are from people you don't know. But I hope you can build an intuitive bridge to both, allowing others' questions to bring your own questions into focus, allowing my answers to suggest new ways of seeking your own answers. This is a theology of the journey, not of the approved question or pat answer.

— ⌒ **Chapter 1** ⌒ —

Church

O preacher, Holy man;
Hear my heart weeping.

QUESTION 1: "Lord, what do you ask of your church?"

Jesus said, "There will be signs in the sun, the moon, and the stars, and on the earth distress among nations confused by the roaring of the sea and the waves." (Luke 21:25)

This was the first question to arrive when I invited readers to join Bartimaeus in asking "questions from the roadside." It came immediately, like a hand reaching out for food or a cry of pain. It reflects "distress" and "confusion" among Christians. It is the question that lies within sea changes in religious affiliation and participation. It helps to explain the astonishing popularity of a novel, *The Da Vinci Code*, about what Jesus might really have intended.

Readers voice distress over the controversies, bickering, threats, and posturing that turn congregational and denominational life into roiling seas but, like ocean water, offer nothing to drink. Readers feel betrayed by systems that talk big but say little, that demand respect but don't offer basic ministries, that know more about spending money than listening to people's cries.

It would be difficult to overstate people's alienation from the church. This isn't trivial, like a liturgical preference or hurt feelings from coffee hour. We are way beyond that. Tinkering and modernizing don't get close to the core sense of betrayal and loss of respect.

One reader sent this statement by a chaplain named Margaret Anderson:

O preacher, Holy man;
Hear my heart weeping.
I long to stand to shout my protests at your sermons.

Where is your power and where is your message?
Where is the gospel of mercy and love?
Your words are nothingness. Nothingness. Nothingness.
We who have come to listen are betrayed.
Servant of God, I am bitter and desolate.
What do I care for perfection of phrases.
Cursed be your humor, your poise, your diction, your theology,
    your dogma.
See how my soul turns to ashes within me.
You who have vowed to declare your Redeemer,
Give me the words that would save.

Clergy get some heat, but only because they are visible projection screens for people's distress. The alienation is broader and deeper. How has a gospel of repentance, light, life, hope, joy, and acceptance devolved into mean-spirited bickering or a bland going through the motions?

If that isn't your question, understand that it is your neighbor's. I mean the neighbor seething next to you, the neighbor begging for acceptance, the absent neighbor who is bound to you only as names on a mailing list.

If it is your question, then know that you are legion.

The answer to the question—"Lord, what do you ask of your Church?"—is this: Pay attention.

Pay attention to people's lives—not their church attendance or their pledge cards, which are at best lagging indicators, but their daily lives. Forget the 1950s, forget the certainties of "old-time religion," forget the easy answers of fundamentalism, forget the inherited structures, forget the way things used to be done, forget the controversies. If we don't know what is actually happening inside people's homes and hearts, if we don't know their names and histories, if we cannot get specific about their anxieties and yearnings, if we cannot sit with them and share the bonding of friendship, if we remain strangers to one another—then we have nothing to say.

Speaking for myself, I am tired of being a name on a list. I get all-clergy mailings from a bishop who has no idea who I am, who has never said a word to me. I get mailings from a congregation where I feel a stranger. I get donation requests from a seminary that thinks preprinted mailers build loyalty.

That isn't ministry. That isn't the body of Christ. That isn't the kingdom of God. That is a lazy, lifeless institution going through the motions. Jesus wanted much more than this.

QUESTION 2: "Does *only* Christianity ensure a home in heaven when we die?" Or, in the words of a second reader, "Are you really sending people to hell because they don't believe in you?"

John said to the crowds that came out to be baptized by him, "You brood of vipers! Who warned you to flee from the wrath to come? Bear fruits worthy of repentance." (Luke 3:7–8)

Surprises mark my day.

At church my spirit sags when a mission speaker carries forward a three-page manuscript. Surprise! His talk is gracious and lively.

A nervous family comes forward to light Advent candles. Surprise! Their words on peace touch me deeply.

At home, we prepare our new house for Christmas. Surprise! We find the window candles and music that we packed a year ago and then moved.

I put on Windham Hill's *Celtic Christmas* CD. Surprise! My appetite for seasonal music hasn't been ruined by "Santa Baby" playing relentlessly at our office building.

While my dad and I check in by phone, my eye moves from study to entryway to dining room. Surprise! Window candles cause the dining room to glow, and I see Christmases past, present, and future filling the room, and they all seem of a piece.

I received many questions about who is saved, who gets to heaven, and is Christianity the only gate to eternal life. I'm not surprised. Over the years, Christians have tried to nail down eternity and have named heaven and hell as theirs to award according to the church's definitions and loyalty oaths.

Who knows? Maybe we can earn our way to heaven by reciting certain words and doing certain deeds. Maybe church doctrine does define God's extent, and clergy do hold the keys to God's kingdom. But I doubt it.

Scripture tells of a God who is infinitely patient and merciful, who loves all of creation, who chastised the Hebrews when they drifted into tribal elitism, who continually surprised the people with a grace and steadfastness that surpassed their own.

Surprises marked the ministry of John the Baptist. He was surprised when people heeded his call to "repentance." They actually listened and came forward for baptism. "Who warned you?" he shouted. Well, in fact, he had warned them, and they had responded.

John was surprised when people asked him to explain salvation. He was surprised when some believed him to be messiah. He was surprised when Jesus of Nazareth stood before him to be baptized.

Like Mary and Joseph when they said Yes to God, John the Baptist was surprised when his Yes changed everything and his life spun out of control. The measure of his faith wasn't his ability to restore order, but his willingness to let himself be swept away.

Church history tells how human efforts to nail down God were confounded again and again by surprising discoveries of new manuscripts, new knowledge, and new ways of serving and seeing God. Is our experience today any less marked by surprise? Travelers and college students discover expressions of faith that aren't like their own and yet seem authentic. New music emerges, and to our surprise, some of it is deep and good. Muslim and Christian stand together in a world made dangerous by religious intolerance and, to their surprise, find common ground and mutual respect.

Some custodians of the Christian franchise reject any such surprises. They demand control and order. They insist on narrow gates and exclusive claims to salvation. They want the answer to be: Yes, Christianity is the only way, and all others will fry in hell.

I think their need for control blinds them to the full story of Scripture. I know that attempts to enforce exclusivity have been brutal and self-serving. I think God is larger than they would allow and certainly more filled with surprises.

Saying our Yes to God doesn't require others to be wrong.

QUESTION 3: "Jesus, what role does the church have in building faith? Your ministry was in the garden, in the valley, in the desert, along the roadside. Where does organized religion fit in? Or does it?"

And the Word became flesh and lived among us, and we have seen his glory, the glory as of a father's only son, full of grace and truth. (John 1:14)

For three years I lived in Gloucester, Massachusetts, in a small shingled house built in 1684. From the back door, I could see weather approaching across Ipswich Bay. From the front, I saw forsythia.

Not just any forsythia, but the wild giant of all forsythia bushes—sprawling, untamed, and fascinating to me in its springtime blaze of yellow.

On weekdays I drove my MGC past the forsythia and down to the train station for my commute to Boston. On Sundays I drove to the local

Episcopal church, where I sang in the choir, assisted with communion, ate occasional dinners at the rector's table, and discovered what John meant by the "glory" of God.

St. John's was a musty church, but to my hungry soul it was "full of grace and truth." Our small choir sounded angelic to my ears. Despite being hounded by a mean vestry, the rector and his wife were saints to me. Our pageants were modest but heartfelt. It was here that I felt a call to ordained ministry.

Today, far from Cape Ann, I will complete my own forsythia project. My wife noticed a landscaper removing forsythia from a nearby property and invited him to leave some uprooted bushes with us. Next spring, from front and back doors, we will see yellow.

Tomorrow, we will take another step into a nearby church. It isn't easy to find a church home. We worshiped in one congregation for three years and loved it, but it was too far from our neighborhood. This new church still feels foreign, but the more we enter in, the more familiar it will feel.

Many readers have asked where "church" fits in. Some have wandered away from former church homes, some have fled in terror or disgust. One pastor asks, "If God is real, why is the church so awful?" Some feel okay about their congregation but loathe denominational politics. Some are confused by religion's changing cultural role. An Englishwoman asks, "Why does religion seem to be dying out in Britain?"

I personally doubt that church, as we know it, is what Jesus had in mind. Religion's concern for hierarchy, power, rules, definitions, solemn assemblies, judging, and excluding aren't at all what Jesus lived. Our typical religious forms—well-tended buildings on well-traveled roads, hotly debated liturgies, and closely monitored clergy—speak reams about the human condition but say little of the wild and restless God who led nomads across the desert. Our religious battles reveal our need for salvation, but not the face of Jesus.

And yet, when it comes to seeing the glory of Jesus, where else shall we look? Family can reveal love, but we also need a love that embraces strangers and outcasts. We need broader circles than our neighborhoods, and loyalties that take us beyond self-interest. At some point, we need that joy which we cannot give ourselves.

The first believers had the Word living among them, and they beheld his glory. We take some solace from stories about that era. But derivative glory never seems enough. We need grace and truth in the flesh. For better or worse, what we have is each other. In the gardens, valleys, deserts, and roadside where we live today, we need a living Word. As "awful" as church can be, we keep turning there in hope, for we need to get outside ourselves.

I can plant forsythia, but I cannot make it grow. I need to be reminded of that, even if the reminder occasionally needs pruning.

QUESTION 4: "Do the differences between our religions and within our religions just represent cultural distortions in our ability to understand and connect to the same God? Are any of us getting close?"

All were questioning in their hearts concerning John, whether he might be the Messiah. (Luke 3:15)

It's lunchtime. A colleague and I face the daily quandary: where to go.

We have the usual eleven restaurants nearby. Three are upscale, two are sports-oriented, four are tolerable, one has an unpleasant proprietor, and one has lost its luster. Some days the selection feels rich, some days uninspiring.

What we choose depends on our starting point. Do we want familiar? Or special? Or speedy? Hovering waiters or room for a business discussion? Are we just hungry, and any place will do?

Some would look at our quandary and say, "Aren't you fortunate to have choices?" Some would say, "Just be glad you have food and can afford it." Some would say, "Move to a real city." Some would say, "Bring your own lunch."

Make the intuitive leap to Sunday or whenever the religious urge strikes. We have the same quandary: where to go, if anywhere.

Some of us live in areas with many choices, such as Christian, Muslim, or Jewish. Within each tradition are many flavors, such as Methodist, Presbyterian, and Baptist. Within each flavor are choices, such as liberal or conservative. Or getting more granular, this conservative church with good music and a strong preacher, or that one two miles away.

In a competitive religious environment, congregations work hard to get us in the door. They spruce up their grounds, enhance their signage, add space when necessary, add staff, add technology, court trendsetters, and train greeters.

Some go farther. To promote brand loyalty, they condemn competitors as infidels or "soft on sin" or insufficiently Bible-based or inadequately "spiritual." They declare themselves righteous and their way the only way. They speak in absolutes, because pride in being right and fear of being wrong are strong motivators. Some promise far more than they can deliver, such as guarantees of eternity.

Even if your congregation stops short of triumphalism, the question tends to remain: In what ways, if any, are we distinct or "right" or uniquely wise? Why would a pilgrim choose us, rather than another church or tradition?

We tend to start at the point of already believing we are special and wanting to understand our right decision. Catechisms aren't so much instructional as affirming. Congregational distinctions focus on what sets us apart from others. Arguments happen, because we are defending our differences.

So, yes, differences among religions sometimes reflect "cultural distortions," to use the reader's term. People tend to segregate into subsets and then to discover religious grounds for doing so.

What would happen, I wonder, if we saw our starting points, not our destinations? What if we saw the expectation and neediness that cause us to care about faith at all? Instead of evaluating the food, what if we experienced our hunger? Instead of defending our choices, what if we examined our need to act?

Starting points are where we tend to have much in common. We may file into different restaurants today, but we started in the common experience of desiring food. Same on Sunday (or Friday or Saturday). We experience a common need for God. We might still enter different houses of prayer, but not with pride in right opinion, rather with gratitude at being free to worship or at having a God who cares.

Christians and Muslims, then, could discover the yearnings they share, rather than the end-point forms and doctrines that separate them. For there is nowhere near as much truth in doctrine as there is in hands reaching out for holy food. Whether those hands reach by name to Yahweh, God, or Allah is probably incidental to the One whose heart sees us reaching.

QUESTION 5: "How can I, as one employed in the institutional church, work in, through, or in spite of it to proclaim a transforming gospel?"

Jesus did this, the first of his signs, in Cana of Galilee, and revealed his glory; and his disciples believed in him. (John 2:11)

Instead of my usual coffee-making routine, today I try something different.

Why? "Change for the sake of change," of course. "Reinventing the wheel," of course. There is always a better way to do something. Routine dulls the senses.

I haul out an old friend: an Italian stovetop espresso maker. Thirty years old, about as low-tech as one can get in brewing coffee.

My adventure has two consequences: First, the contraption makes a mess, reminding me why I stopped using it. Second, it makes a great pot of coffee. Maybe good flavor requires a mess.

This morning, across the Christian landscape, preachers will stand before their people and face the same opportunity and danger. Whether they speak long or short, from lofty pulpit or ground level, they will face an ambiguous, complex environment that can daunt even the strongest.

The audience will include friends, enemies, and strangers, the open-minded and the skeptical. Some will listen for guidance and inspiration; others for shortcomings, as if they were drama critics gauging a performance. Some will do little more than time the sermon. Some will compare it with a predecessor's efforts. Many, in these combative times, will listen for proof of orthodoxy. Some will tune out immediately.

Preachers realize that Jesus faced the same hurdles. And look what happened to him. These people are, after all, one's employers. Many preachers will join today's reader in asking how they can present a "transforming gospel" in an environment that is profoundly conservative, where institutional change is viewed as violation and personal change as threat.

My answer is, Make a mess. By that I don't mean shock value, clever stories, props, or any of the attention-getting behaviors that convince laity their clergy are immature and irrelevant.

I mean preach as if life depended on it. See the pain out there, and preach to it, even if the hurting are trying to hide from their pain. See the smugness, and preach to it. See all of the defenses that people use against God, and preach to them.

I mean know the questions that truly engage people's hearts and minds—not the polite questions they asked on arriving, but the questions that greeted them on awakening—and preach to those questions, knowing, as Jesus knew, that truth and hope lie within the clouds of parable and not within the faux clarity of law and doctrine.

I mean turn on the heat and not know exactly what will come of it. Trust God to finish the brew. Trust God to take an honest word and use it for good purpose. If yesterday's pot seemed bland, don't do it that way today, even though it is safe.

A preacher's critics will always find cause for fault; they live to find fault. They aren't today's audience. They might be tomorrow's, when life has undercut their smugness. For now, give bread to the hungry.

Jesus didn't show his glory by doing the polite, safe, or predictable thing. He saw actual need and responded to it. That, as I see it, is the heart of preaching: seeing needs and preaching to them. It isn't style, cleverness, erudition, or entertainment values. It isn't even biblical scholarship, for the Word comes alive in the telling, not in the analyzing.

The heart of preaching is to look on these well-dressed, change-resistant, polite employers and to see them, not as they see themselves, but as God sees them. The result will be a mess, both tears on cheeks and glare in eyes. But better to go down in the mess—possibly the flames—of trying than to protect a paycheck by offering thin brew.

QUESTION 6: "I am a new church start pastor working with those who have been 'de-churched.' How can we help each other see beyond the pain inflicted by human communities to see the community in Christ we can be?"

Jesus began to say to the people of Nazareth, "Today this scripture has been fulfilled in your hearing." All spoke well of him and were amazed at the gracious words that came from his mouth. They said, "Is not this Joseph's son?" (Luke 4:21–22)

Democratic candidates eviscerate each other. Republican incumbents wait their turn. By November, every candidate will have been labeled, exposed, and smeared.

Every failing will be paraded, going back to childhood, as if personal growth were impossible. Every course correction will be noted, as if learning by experience didn't change anything.

Is it any wonder that politicians develop thick skins, hide their motivations, and surround themselves with sycophants? Is it any wonder that people sanitize their resumes and histories to hide failure or weakness?

In my years as a pastor, it never ceased to amaze me how cruel people could be. They would say and do anything to get their way. They would grind their pastors into dust if that promised an extra measure of control. They would berate fellow parishioners to make their own worlds safer.

It isn't just the church, of course. Office politics and school politics can be just as cruel. People attack and then hide behind some "greater good." If not God's will, then some theory, entitlement, or alleged purpose. Any flag will do as we exercise our need to be mean.

If that seems unfairly harsh, visit any group that serves the wounded. Today's reader refers to his congregation as the "de-churched" and his ministry as response to pain. Listen to clergy when they dare to be honest. Listen to their spouses. Talk to lay leaders about their experiences. Talk to teachers about parents. Talk to the estimated 25 percent of girls who suffer incest, or the 10 percent who get raped in college, or the boys who have comparable experiences but, in an odd double standard, endure even greater shame.

Sure, some things are worse than others. Schoolyard name-calling is a far cry from selling Russian girls into slavery in California. But they are all of a piece. They are gradations of a human phenomenon that Jesus addressed head on and, in what God hoped would be a lesson to us all, became its victim.

It started small. Jesus spoke a word that his townsfolk found gracious but unsettling. They questioned his worthiness. How could a carpenter's son have such wisdom? But Jesus forged on. He had already named them as poor, captive, and blind. Now he named their hypocrisy. They tried to kill him.

His ministry became a two-edged sword. Minister to the wounded and outcast, and tell hard truth to those who caused such suffering. It was a confusing ministry, because most people experience both sides of the coin: they get hurt, and they hurt others. Jesus seemed to love with one hand and to chastise with the other.

The issues, it seems to me, are control and safety.

We seem to feel a visceral need to control—control other people, control our surroundings. Lack of control is perceived as dangerous, as a sign of weakness.

Our quest for safety goes beyond physical security. We want protection against change, new ideas, uncomfortable truth, strangers, and honesty.

To gain control and safety, we fire at will. Not even family or faith community is safe ground. In our desperation, we hurt even those we love.

How can we change this? It has to start in a personal decision not to hurt another. Risk noncontrol, risk danger, but stop the cycle of pain, resist the temptation to fire back, love the enemy, and accept suffering on behalf of others as a calling, not a mistake.

QUESTION 7: "Jesus, what does turning the other cheek, being persecuted for your name, and bearing a cross look like right now in my church (Episcopal) and my world?"

Jesus said, "Truly I tell you, no prophet is accepted in the prophet's hometown." (Luke 4:24)

From my seeing point—indoors, early-morning light, top of a hill—our steep driveway looks passable, thanks to snow shoveling yesterday.

But is that enough seeing? Yes, I'm ready to return to work. But do I want to start a 3,000-pound car down an incline without testing the surface?

Even then, I have more to see. How bad is ice around the corner? How about main roads? How about other drivers, many of them falsely feeling secure in SUVs? I am not normally hesitant in driving. But these aren't normal conditions. No matter how eager I am for work, 60 MPH in heavy traffic isn't the time to discover ice.

In these uncertain times, too many believers are barreling down the highway as if they'd already seen enough. As diversity challenges former worldviews, as new ways walk alongside old ways, as change threatens the settled, strong reactions are occurring. Like a type A personality reeling under cabin fever, many believers are saying, "Enough of this!" They roar their engines, point the car where they want to go, and speed away.

They condemn the divergent—not just disagree, but condemn as "evil." They reject the normal decision-making processes—not just regroup for another vote, but reject as demonic. They refuse to compromise, because their house-of-cards belief structure would collapse. They conspire to cripple and to destroy, because their certainty requires victory at any cost. They throw out accusations and labels without regard to whom they wound.

They think themselves prophets of our time, brave and righteous. In fact, they are blinded by rage, fear, bigotry, and pride.

Or so I see it. I find these sad and frightening times in religion. But I could be wrong. I might not be seeing enough.

And that, I think, is the reality we must all accept, or else be trapped in self-destruction. We might all be wrong. We might all be not seeing enough. No matter how eager we are to usher in a new age or to prevent that new age, we might be blind. Taking votes doesn't improve our vision, nor does rejecting those votes. Tossing Scriptures at one another doesn't uncloud our eyes. And passing resolutions merely draws the blindfold tighter.

Jesus understood himself as a prophet. What he meant by that is unclear. The age of prophets came early in the old covenant era and was complex and changeable, from a primitive anointing of kings to raging against the self-serving, from a detailed accounting of the nation's sins to dreamy visions of better days.

But the root was seeing. A prophet was a "seer," not a foreteller of tomorrow, but a clear-eyed, unflinching observer of today. John the Baptist saw the hypocrisy of his people. Jesus saw their wounds and fears. What they saw made them unpopular and angry. But anger and unpopularity aren't the measure of a prophet. The heart of prophecy is always God-given sight, as opposed to blindness.

A reader asks what cross bearing looks like in these troubled times. I think it means a humble admission of our own blindness. We don't see enough. We might hold the keys to this car, but we are fools to barrel down the hill as if the laws of gravity and friction didn't apply to us.

We tear apart our churches and tear into each other, as if we had seen enough to know truth. We are wrong about that. And we might be wrong about a whole lot else. Faith, it seems to me, compels us to stop fulminating and to admit the possibility that we don't see enough to be driving with such certainty.

QUESTION 8: "Jesus, what do you think of this religion, Christianity?"

Just as Moses and Elijah were leaving Jesus, Peter said to Jesus, "Master, it is good for us to be here; let us make three dwellings, one for you, one for Moses, and one for Elijah"—not knowing what he said. (Luke 9:33)

I drive my son to church for a confirmation class trip to a Jewish synagogue. On the way my father calls and tells me about a visit by a fellow widower. His son, a childhood friend, wasn't allowed to swim with us because our club barred Jews.

The confirmation teacher gives an idle, inaccurate, and shallow description of what we will see at the synagogue, which she insists on calling "church." No spark, no preparation, no reason for anyone to care.

At the synagogue, I sit with three boys and explain the service. Their eyes open wide as people sing, bend the knee, bow, sway, and pray in Hebrew and English.

The rabbi speaks somberly about a march that American Nazis and the Ku Klux Klan will make today in our state's capital. Anti-Semitism is on the rise, he says. A tall man wearing a prayer scarf says words that Jesus said but hardly anyone ever repeats.

"Pray for those who hate us."

In six words this man offers a better sermon than anything I have heard in church in years. Such focus, such clarity.

A woman comes forward to sing and sign a closing prayer. "Sh'ma, Yisrael," she begins, her hands making the sign for "listen." "Hear, Israel, the Lord our God is one."

Afterward, the rabbi meets with us. He is prepared. He teaches. He cares about our being there. Our children ask few questions. They don't seem to notice the astounding grace of a prayer for one's enemies or an ancient cry shattering today's calm.

At home, I check e-mail. One tells of a priest being driven from her church—a complicated story, not all one-sided—and of formerly vibrant congregations slowly dying, living off endowments, drifting and floating, in a city that has doubled in size in recent years. Another tells of a church being starved by angry parishioners, because of the denomination's refusal to hate gays—this in the city where Nazis and Klansmen will march today.

What does Jesus think about the religion claiming his name? I imagine Jesus standing with Moses and Elijah, hearing about the wilderness wandering and the tragedy of Israel's kings. "Sh'ma, Jehoshua, Adonai Elohaynu Adonai Echad." I imagine Jesus taking heart from those who have gone before.

I imagine Jesus turning to his friends and hearing his beloved Simon say the words that would echo forward through the years, floating easily off the tongues of power-seeking bishops and emperors, proud intellectuals, haters of strangers, those movers and shakers who use faith to claim an earthly footstool, the fearful and controlling, the teachers who don't prepare, the preachers who don't give their flocks anything to care about, the manipulators of money.

These words: "It is good for us to be here; let us make dwellings."

I imagine Jesus starting to die inside at that very moment. I imagine Jesus still dying, because we cannot muster the energy to care, we cannot let go of control, we cannot master our impulse to hate, we cannot see beyond our walls to a city square just blocks away where evil will parade while we obsess about sex.

I hear a sigh deeper than any sadness we could know. I see God lifting hands to ears and then sliding them forward in Moses' ancient plea: "Sh'ma, Yisrael, Adonai Elohaynu Adonai Echad."

I imagine Jesus looking at the proud and self-serving institution we have created and seeing our unconcern. We build, rather than listen. We fight, rather than serve. We try to please, rather than have a faith that evil would find daunting.

QUESTION 9: "How can we create the church into a loving, caring institution?"

While Peter was saying this, a cloud came and overshadowed them; and they were terrified as they entered the cloud. Then from the cloud came a voice that said, "This is my Son, my Chosen; listen to him!" When the voice had spoken, Jesus was found alone. (Luke 9:34–36)

In much of Christianity, today is church day. A few will provide— leading worship, greeting, teaching, singing—and many will receive.

Most will go home wondering if they gave or received enough. For it is the nature of the religious enterprise to yearn for more, to ask, in the melancholy words of singer Peggy Lee, "Is that all there is?"

Preachers will wonder: Did I connect? Did I say all that needed to be said? Their congregations will wonder: Was there more? In a well-organized church, greeters will enter tracking data and trigger a visitor-response system, grounded in a need to embrace persons. A poorly organized church won't notice and respond, and visitors will go home crushed, perhaps bearing a coffee mug advertising the name of the church.

Teachers will wonder if anything worthwhile just happened. Students will rejoin the Sunday treadmill, in some cases wondering: What more could I have learned?

If this were a retail business, the owner would study the data—hard data like receipts and customer count, and soft data like feedback and intuition. Church leaders usually recoil at such business analogies. They believe theirs is holier work. I suspect they just don't want to study the data, for it will be too chastening. I remember getting hammered by a vestry for the simple act of counting people accurately. They had been lying to themselves for years.

A reader asks how we can create a "loving, caring institution." I think today's conclusion of the Transfiguration story suggests two answers.

The first is to be "terrified" in the Sunday-morning cloud, not smug or comfortable. Sunday morning will always be a cloud filled with yearnings, moods, and needs. If we saw that cloud settling over us—sadness, grieving, crumbling marriage, angry teenager, nervous newcomer—we would be frightened of the awesome responsibility thrust upon us. If we knew what was at stake in this hour of worship, we would fall to our knees.

But we don't. Or not enough do. I understand why. It is a scary thing to stand in the pulpit, to see the neediness out there, and to wonder if today is the day to jettison pulpit and sermon, and to stand among the people, like Jesus on the plain, to proclaim good news.

More should feel that terror. Greeters, singers, readers—all should feel it. Not stage fright at performing, but the weight of responsibility. Would readers treat Scripture so casually if they knew what was at stake?

Second, we need to let the cloud be lifted—not cling to the delusion called "respecting tradition"—and to see Jesus standing alone, bidding us walk down the mountain with him. If we looked into his eyes and saw his lonely compassion, how could we freeze out a newcomer, offer a half-hearted class, or bicker in the parking lot? If we understood what lies below—Jerusalem, life through dying, hope through suffering—how could we be so casual about our time together?

We need accountability. Shared accountability—not the clergy's alone, not a report card at salary-setting time. But all Sunday ministry providers sensing what is at stake and taking their duties seriously.

Eventually, one can dream of an entire congregation committed to effective servanthood. But that's too much for now. It has to start with leadership. Do parish leaders want to "be in business," to do the difficult work of succeeding at ministry? If they do, every ministry provider needs to accept accountability—starting with the terrifying awareness that this is real, it matters, lives are at stake.

QUESTION 10: "Would it be so bad if organized religion blew itself out of the water, back to the simplicity of two thousand years ago with no churches to eat up all the alms in maintenance and salaries? What right-minded person would want to belong to a church like ours?"

> *Jesus said, "How often have I desired to gather your children together as a hen gathers her brood under her wings, and you were not willing!"* (Luke 13:34)

Another reader put her question even more succinctly: "If God is real, why is the church so awful?"

I suspect we have all asked such questions from time to time. After a shallow sermon, after an endless annual meeting, after a leadership conflict, when a pastoral crisis was overlooked or a hospital visit seemed insincere, when a reader was unprepared or a choir uninterested, when denominational affairs waxed nonsensical, when prelates pranced better than they preached, when stories of abuse or thievery broke the Sunday calm—on these and other occasions we have asked: Is this the best we can do?

Some blame religious leaders. One reader asked: "Why have our religious leaders bound up so many of their followers and made their life so miserable?" Some blame institutional pride, as in this reader's question: "Why does each church continue to build a giant edifice, costing millions of dollars, when this country is rapidly descending into third world nation status?" Some blame men. Some blame women. Some blame raging fundamentalism. Some blame liberals. Some blame themselves.

We need to know that such questions are rampant. Even if our experience is different and our congregation is wonderful, we need to know why "None" is the fastest-growing religious preference in the U.S., why church participation is nearing zero in much of Europe, why giving is down and attendance is half-hearted.

If I had a simple remedy, I would offer it. In recent years congregations have tried spiritual renewal, intensive Bible study, lay academies, new liturgies, new music, gender shifts, church-growth methodologies, small groups, rigid theology and easygoing theology, free food, and paved parking lots. Each effort works for a while, but then familiar forces return, such as lethargy, despair, bickering.

I don't think people are any less hungry for God. If anything, the vexing complexities of modern life and events like 9/11 have sharpened our hunger. But something about our lives as the "gathered" of God isn't working. For many? For most? I don't know, but for enough that we all ought to be concerned.

Jesus voiced his desire to "gather [God's] children together as a hen gathers her brood under her wings." Whatever institutional shape we give to it, the foundational fact is that God desires to gather people. In open fields or supermarket aisles, in grand cathedrals or humble country clapboard, God is a gatherer.

In order to gather, God liberates people from bondage; breaks down walls like class, ethnicity, and gender; and enables a common language of joy and sadness.

Jesus goes on to cry out, however: "and you were not willing!" This is what turns God's desire to lamentation. God would gather, we would hide. God would liberate, we would enslave. God would break down walls, we would build them higher (and call them God's walls!). What

God would do we aren't willing to allow. What God would give we aren't willing to receive. What God would say we aren't willing to hear.

These aren't matters that any institution can resolve. It may be we've expected too much of our churches. Instead of looking for God in laws or traditions, in doctrines or clergy, in buildings or budgets, we should look for God in the gathering—however flawed the gathering might be.

If we saw our yearnings and celebrated our small glimpse of grace, the trappings would lose their ability to captivate or distress us.

QUESTION 11: "Is there a way for a female to find the way to God in our current male-biased denominations without leaving the church altogether?"

[Jesus said, "The elder son] became angry and refused to go in. His father came out and began to plead with him. But he answered his father, "Listen! For all these years I have been working like a slave for you, and I have never disobeyed your command; yet you have never given me even a young goat so that I might celebrate with my friends." (Luke 15:28–29)

Every time I think we have left former days behind, I receive a reminder like an e-mail I received today commending moviemaker Mel Gibson for his "political battle against Jewish Movie Mega owners" and "money hungry, morally corrupt liberals."

What a "tidy package of bigotry," I responded.

As a white male, I am only occasionally on the receiving end of gender or racial bigotry. The bigotry I have experienced—anticlerical, antiliberal—is comparable, but probably not as painful.

Bigotry takes several forms. One is scapegoating—humankind's tragic tendency to blame one group for all woes. Another is rejection based on otherness—skin color, for example—with no desire to know the others at any depth, in the uniqueness of their personality and experience. Another hides behind politeness. Another is like a terrorist sleeper cell—such as an explosion of racist rage in a traffic snarl or the anti-immigrant explosions after the terrorist attacks in September 2001—well hidden, even to oneself, until something triggers a blast of hatred.

There is another form that bigotry takes, and it might be the most confusing. It's the dilemma exemplified by the elder son in Jesus' parable. It is, I believe, the dilemma voiced by the reader who asks if women can ever find a place in the church.

The elder son got there first. He had that assurance of place that first-born children tend to have. He also behaved responsibly, as first-born children tend to do. He saw the father's requirements—in the way first-borns tend to identify with the father—and he lived into them.

He was deeply offended, therefore, when the younger son received the father's extravagant love and celebration. How could they possibly be equal in the father's eyes? How could the younger son be given what he himself had had to earn? How could irresponsibility merit the same love as responsibility?

Maybe the elder son of Jesus' parable was just a bigoted jerk. Many people are. But I think of him mainly as confused, in the way first-born children are confused by new siblings, and first-arrivals are confused by late-arrivals, and longtime members are confused by newcomers, and established citizens are confused by immigrants, and men who welcome women into leadership roles are confused by how different things then seem.

His confusion took the form of anger—that perfect cover for other emotions—and if he had gotten his way, the prodigal son would have been punished first, before being allowed home. I don't condone his response, but having witnessed sibling rivalry among my own children and huge tensions between old-timers and newcomers in every church I served, I do understand it.

The answer to the reader's question, I think, is a tentative Yes. There is a way for women to feel at home in denominations that were, or still are, dominated by men. In the same way, gays can feel at home, minorities can feel at home, and newcomers can feel at home. But it won't be easy.

The burden of understanding will fall on all parties. The "elder sons" among us need to understand who the new arrivals are, and why they deserve God's welcome and yet why their arrival feels so confusing, perhaps unwelcome. Those seeking to enter or to take new roles need to understand why it is okay for them to upset a stable order—but also why they cannot simply displace the elder sons, but must learn who they are and form community with them.

QUESTION 12: "How can we nurture our flock and equip them to serve at the same time? How do we feed the sheep and, at the same time, ask the sheep to work for the other sheep? Is this possible?"

When the scribes and chief priests realized that [Jesus] had told this parable against them, they wanted to lay hands on him at that very hour, but they feared the people. (Luke 20:19)

This morning pastors will stand before their flocks and be afraid.

They fear rejection. They fear tangible efforts to deprive them of employment and intangible efforts to intimidate them into compliance. They fear the ecclesiastical equivalent of a plant closing, as energy flows elsewhere. Like a shop owner competing with Wal-Mart, they wonder how long their gray-haired, change-resistant congregation can keep going.

How many are afraid? At least 25 percent are engaged in active leadership conflicts. My guess is that another 25 percent worry that they could be next, and another 25 percent nervously scan the faces of their parishioners for frowns, boredom, any sign of alienation.

A fearful pastor isn't likely to be an effective pastor. How does one preach a life-transforming gospel to people who are inches from terminating one's paycheck? How does one provide pastoral care—an exercise grounded not in niceness and smiles but in a bold engagement with reality—when denial of reality is rampant? How does one plan creatively for the future when any future that isn't a continuation of the present is seen as betrayal? How does a pastor speak from the heart—a place, inevitably, of questioning, doubt, turmoil, pain, discovery, and joy—when higher value is placed on certainty and decorum?

Parishioners, therefore, aren't untouched by their pastors' fears. Preaching will seem safe and bland—and therefore uninteresting, unenlightening. Pastoral attention will be inconsistent, not because clergy don't care, but because they are trapped in budget meetings, planning workshops, conflict sessions, outside consultants. The enterprise will seem flat and routine, because that risky vigor that was the hallmark of Jesus' ministry has become too dangerous. The enterprise will feel like a favorite store that isn't making it.

A reader asks about strategies for dealing with "burnout" among key laity, who want only to be left alone, and asks how to feed and nurture a flock, not in the abstract of pastoral theory, but in the reality of weariness, boredom, and stress.

My answer isn't another round of strategizing on parish development or training. We can't intellectualize our way out of this. Nor is my answer a venture into some "ism," some cause that temporarily focuses our energies in right opinion.

I think we need to name our hungers and make them our business.

Most clergy are hungry to serve. They didn't go into ordained ministry for the pay. They went because their lives were touched by God in some way. I think clergy need to own that hunger and minister from it. Laity squander an important resource when they stifle their clergy in order to make their worlds temporarily safer.

Laity are hungry, too, and their hungers have little to do with liturgical style, tradition, bishops' pronouncements, church controversies, or property. People are dealing with illness and death, economic displacement, warfare, addictions, failing marriages, frustrating relationships, and loneliness. Property committee meetings and denominational arguments are a sorry response to a hunger to be known, loved, and valued.

I think we need to stop blaming one another, as if someone must take the role assigned to the scribes and chief priests, the bad guys in the story, the ones against whom Jesus speaks, the ones who conspire against God.

I think we should simplify our churches: pastors preaching from their hearts about the gospel that touches their lives, parishioners listening and asking their own questions, everyone coming to see one another as hungry, worthy, a child of God.

It's time for more focus on people and less on institution.

Chapter 2

Suffering

QUESTION 13: "Do You ever despair or weep that you began this whole thing?"

[Jesus said,] "Now when these things begin to take place, stand up and raise your heads, because your redemption is drawing near." (Luke 21:28)

It is a day of comings and goings.

Around noon, second son arrives bearing cheese and crackers for the holiday spread. Soon, first son and his girlfriend arrive bearing more snacks and designer water. While the turkey bakes, three generations nibble and connect.

Snack time over, three sons and girlfriend play basketball. I watch them from the dining room window: so young, so healthy, so exuberant, so much of life ahead of them. Whatever we share today, they will continue tomorrow in other times and places.

After a marvelous feast, we walk the one-mile loop, pairing off for quiet conversation on a road flanked by empty trees. As always in our family, conversation tends to be, "What next," rather than, "Remember when."

After two kinds of pie, we gather in the living room, two to read, five to play poker, then Scrabble. (I have the letters for GIVER and am searching for an open E to create GRIEVE, when I notice an A and use all seven letters for AVERRING and a score of 89 points.)

After games and a telephone report about my parents' Thanksgiving Day, my boys ask about the bedtime stories I used to tell, with homemade characters like Squire Squirrel and Arthur the Airedale Dog.

I remember New Hampshire vacations, when we lay on the floor for the latest adventures of Milford Cabinet and his animal friends.

I check e-mail and discover more details about the gathering of family next month in Indianapolis. Saying farewell to my mother seems closer than it was, and we who return to other places will celebrate all that was given us.

We all respond differently to life's comings and goings. How could we not be ambivalent about admiring our children and yet feeling sad at their growing up and going onward? How could we not be smiling and tearful at remembering the bedtime stories we were told and watching the storytellers move on to larger life?

Some try to cling, even though onward never stops. Some see only the absence and not the fullness that is being shared elsewhere now. Some feel alone—too many goings. Some rejoice over continuations that they believe in but will never see. Most of us probably whipsaw between hearing the laughter and fearing the silence.

I wish I had written down the story I told on a summer's evening in New Hampshire. But it never occurred to me that death was drawing near to this family, that the farmhouse would pass into younger hands, that boys would become men, and I would cross so many sands that the sound of Squire Squirrel's voice would be lost to me.

But I told the story once, and it warmed a cool night. Some day those boys will tell stories to other children—their own stories, their own wager on tomorrow.

No, Jesus doesn't despair at what he began. These comings and goings—that he, too, experienced—aren't a contradiction of life. They are life. They are what Jesus came to ennoble and to redeem. He, too, turned one direction to see life passing away and then the other to see life charging exuberantly onward.

"Stand up and raise your heads," he said. Not a single act of this drama is wasted or undeserving. Even the sadness is worthy, even the leave-taking, even the empty chair.

Yes, Jesus does weep. If love be at all kindled, it must shed tears from time to time. The feast must end, the day of together must give way to apart, bedtime can only be delayed so long. Then the storyteller names the moral, kisses each child, forgets the words just spoken but remembers the love.

QUESTION 14: "Why wouldn't you let me feel you or know that you were there during my dark nights of the soul?"

As it is written in the book of the words of the prophet Isaiah, "The voice of one crying out in the wilderness: 'Prepare the way of the Lord, make his paths straight.'" (Luke 3:4)

Sleep proves elusive.

Much is on my mind: illness up north, situations at work, plus a backdrop of war and political turmoil.

I wouldn't characterize this as a truly "dark night of the soul." I've had darker. But the sensation is familiar: mind swirling, emotions unsettled, questions popping up but not staying long enough to be answered, listening to the night sounds.

I doubt that any two sleepless nights are identical. Life brings an infinite variety of pain, doubt, and loss. We are sturdier some days than others, more or less vulnerable, more or less content with ourselves.

But our common ground in such moments might be known as "exile."

It is exile that explains why Jesus came, served, died, and rose again. Yet it is exile that we resist seeing. We prefer to talk of law, institution, righteousness, and victory, as if the messianic moment were the anointing of one tribe to rule all tribes, and the primary aim of faith were correctness.

The Old Testament era had several pivotal moments: the calling of Abraham, the exodus from Egypt, the settling of Canaan, and the founding of Jerusalem. But none was as searing and central as exile. For in being deported to Assyria and later to Babylon, the Hebrews lost touch with a God whom they had rooted too deeply in the land. "How," they asked, "shall we sing the Lord's song upon an alien soil?"

During the exile in Babylon, the Hebrews changed. They made peace with their captors, discovered how to worship away from the temple, and came to consider Babylon their home. When Cyrus king of Persia set them free to return home, most didn't want to leave. As far as they knew, they were home.

That is the context for the songs and images of messiah. Not a new lawgiver like Moses, not a new king like David, but a redeemer who would find his people in exile and lead them home. But what if they didn't want to go home? That was the quandary that led Isaiah to sing:

Comfort, O comfort my people,
Speak tenderly to Jerusalem,
"In the wilderness prepare the way of the LORD." (Isa. 40:1)

The exiles wouldn't leave of their own accord. They needed a redeemer to come to them, to take them by the hand and to tame the desert.

This is how John the Baptist understood Jesus: a redeemer of exiles. And that is how John understood the human condition: exile. Defeated in battle by overwhelming forces, led away captive, making peace with our captors, forgetting where home is, terrified of the unknown, willing to remain in exile.

That wasn't a self-understanding that early Christians wanted to embrace. They preferred to see themselves as a holy tribe feasting on a new paschal Lamb, as God's elect called to rule, as a righteous remnant that would save humanity from sin, as builders of a new Jerusalem.

Those were pleasing images and energizing. But they missed the larger point of redemption from exile. They left us not knowing ourselves—exiles, not rulers in training—and not recognizing messiah when he draws near.

I don't know what caused this reader's dark night, or why God felt absent at that moment. But I do believe that God sends a redeemer to lead us home, and that our starting point is exile and our destination will be foreign to us. Does that make the dark night shorter or lighter? Probably not. But it might help us to hear the tender voice of one coming to find us.

QUESTION 15: "I would shout to Jesus, 'Have you seen my father? Is he OK? Please tell me that by the grace of God he's OK now. Have you seen my father? He suffered here so long.'"

John said, "Every valley shall be filled, and every mountain and hill shall be made low, and the crooked shall be made straight, and the rough ways made smooth." (Luke 3:5)

I have no immediate analogy to this man's question. I have no anecdote that builds a bridge to his experience of standing alone at graveside, burying a father who "had a rough life," struggled with addiction, and "died with no true friends and not a penny to his name."

I haven't yet buried a parent, although that day isn't far off. I am not estranged from my parents. Their friendships far surpass my own. After too many moves in my own career path, I wonder sometimes who would come to my funeral. But that isn't the issue posed by this man's question.

Sometimes it is enough to know that someone else has suffered. I don't have to understand it firsthand. I don't have to "walk in his shoes." The words, "I know what you mean," are merely a way to distance myself. "Topping" the other's story with a story of my own is cruel. Finding satisfaction in not having suffered like that—as in, "There but for the grace of God go I"—can make me shallow and smug.

Sometimes I just need to see the suffering, hear the story, allow the other to have a unique experience that has nothing to do with me. I am not the center of the universe.

Sometimes it is enough just to listen, to step close to another's pain, to taste the salt of their tears or the acid of their bitterness. It is enough to see eyes that dare not see back, that cannot rise to a hopeful horizon, not yet. It is enough to respect the isolation of one who isn't ready for a soothing hug.

Sometimes it is enough just to let the other be—even though his exile terrifies me, for it exposes mountains that are too high, desert places that are too rough. I cannot make my world safe by rescuing him. Compulsive caregivers don't necessarily give care.

When I draw near to someone in exile, I need to ask, What mountain am I afraid to see? What desert keeps me from getting close or makes me compulsive about forcing closeness? Can I just listen and love, and leave myself out of the transaction?

When the prophet Isaiah sang of exiles returning home—and thereby explained humanity's condition and Jesus as our Redeemer—he told how valleys would be "lifted up," mountains "made low," and "rough places a plain." Like a civil engineer, he imagined the foreboding desert between Babylon and Jerusalem being transformed into a "highway."

He saw more. He saw exiles marching home together, the strong caring for the weak, as a shepherd will "gather the lambs . . . in his bosom, and gently lead the mother sheep." He saw the women of Zion climbing the mountain to see the procession of returning exiles and shouting for joy, for they, too, were in exile. The trees would clap their hands, for they, too, were in exile.

Is this reader's father okay ? I believe so. I believe the gates of larger life are open to all, sinner and saint alike, as maddening as that might be for those who are banking on righteousness.

But the point isn't whether I see the way home accurately, for our doctrines and definitions are like withering grass. The point is that a simple question—what do you need?—touched an exile. "Your question made me weep," he writes. "I didn't know that this was weighing on me until now."

We transform the desert when we ask and listen.

QUESTION 16: "Why was our grandson born prematurely to endure 27 days of suffering before his death?"

In those days Mary set out and went with haste to a Judean town in the hill country, where she entered the house of Zechariah and greeted Elizabeth. (Luke 1:39)

INDIANAPOLIS—I return to my wife and sons today. That means leaving the city of my childhood and saying good-bye to the mother who gave me life. My next visit probably will be for her funeral.

I try to imagine what it means to bear life. I imagine my mother's excitement—first child, new stage in a young marriage, a belief in tomorrow beyond the long war.

I imagine her fears—so young, so far from home, living on an army base, her mother elsewhere, plus the doubts inherent in pregnancy. What if something goes wrong? There are no guarantees in pregnancy, childbirth, or parenthood.

So we wish for luck, or prayers, or peace, or faith, or hope—for that which we cannot give to ourselves.

We make that same wish throughout life, at every stage of this challenging journey, and again as death nears. So little has ever been in our control. So much depends on a God who loves all things, who bears all things, who isn't deterred by our weakness, who sees us coming and rejoices.

I accept it that Mary the mother of Jesus was the unique source of Luke's Gospel. Toward the end of her life, she told him about the early years. She told him about becoming pregnant and rushing to her cousin Elizabeth, also pregnant, for mutual support. Luke cast her story in epic terms, for he knew its outcome and was searching for large meanings. I suspect Mary remembered being young and afraid.

I remember when my wife announced her first pregnancy. The women of our church immediately began to tell her about every difficult pregnancy, labor, and childbirth they had experienced. They weren't being cruel, although it did frighten her. They were naming the risks and pain inherent in motherhood. They were welcoming her to the tribe.

My mother was fortunate. So was my wife. So was Mary. They saw their offspring into adulthood, although not without pain or vexation.

Not every mother is so fortunate. Today's reader asks a wrenching question about extreme misfortune. I am sure every mother and grand-mother cringes just reading it.

For her "Why," there is no answer. There is only the instinctive hug, the grimace, the shared sadness—especially from that tribe who know such things happen and live in dread of them.

I imagine that is why Mary ran to Elizabeth. Not to set up Luke's theological point about the primacy of Jesus over John, or to link Mary to Hannah, mother of the prophet Samuel, but as one woman seeking another as new life began.

I think we find ourselves in other such tribes: the divorced, abused, widows and widowers, parents who lost children, families who lost someone to warfare, beaten-up clergy, the laid-off, and others. I am now part of that tribe which sits with parents as they die. Many of you have written me, because you are in that tribe, too.

Maybe an answer to the reader's question lies in tribal identity. She knows something that few other grandparents know. She is different for it, wounded and yet gifted with a truer word than another might speak. God can use that word, if only to cut through the glibness and pastel phrases that we sometimes use to hide from death.

As we gathered to kiss our mother good-bye, my sister, brother, and I took on a new word, a truer word than we knew before. What we do with that word remains to be seen. But we now have a deeper bond to each other, and to a world where parents die and families change.

QUESTION 17: "Jesus, where do you feel vulnerable in your calling? How do you manage fear and loneliness?"

[When Joseph] heard that Archelaus was ruling over Judea in place of his father Herod, he was afraid to go there. And after being warned in a dream, he went away to the district of Galilee. (Matthew 2:22)

As my mother's dying time nears, the pace of telephone calls picks up.

Two days ago, my brother in Seattle found me on the 4th fairway. With no foursome pressing from behind, I was able to chat freely. Yesterday, my dad found me on the 16th fairway, again with no one coming up behind, again able to talk. Last night, my sister found me closing up the house for the night.

I am a cliché I suppose, and some stipulation of golf etiquette probably says to keep cell phones off the course. But these are important calls, and I intend to take them. I am glad technology makes it possible.

More calls will come today, I imagine. Who knows where they will find me? Taking down the Christmas tree, perhaps, eating with my family, writing a book proposal, maybe even back on the golf course.

If you decide to love, there is no "safe" haven, no place beyond vulnerability. Even though I turned off my cell phone when entering a movie theater last evening, I turned it on immediately afterward and would have been sorry to miss a family call.

Nor would I want such safety. The whole point of loving is to connect, to make oneself available to the other, to lay down one's life for another. Conditional love might preserve escape routes, but the genuine article lays oneself bare. How else could love happen?

In business they talk of "exit strategy," keeping one's résumé up to date, not getting too close to colleagues, not touching each other's lives too deeply. In business, such boundaries are appropriate. But real life and real love are different. We might take "respite," but not "exit." We might take a break, but not break contact. We might remember to "take care of yourself," as the pastoral platitude puts it, but in the end, self ends up suffering anyway. For love leads inexorably to suffering. That's just the way it is.

Joseph bought a brief time of safety for his family in Egypt. When he returned to Israel and found his enemy's son on the throne, he sought safety in Galilee. It lasted for a while, but in time, Jesus made himself vulnerable to his townsfolk in Nazareth and almost was killed. Later, in a ministry shortened by opposition, he made himself vulnerable again and again, in ways small and large, always in love, always knowing that the forces of darkness would find him. But if he wanted the wounded to find him and the needy, then he had to leave a door open for evil, as well.

Where did Jesus feel vulnerable in his calling? Everywhere, I imagine. In crowds, he faced people who would be threatened by his teachings and healings. With his disciples, he faced their obtuseness and pride. With his parents and siblings, he faced the limits of their comprehension. Even alone in prayer, he faced a God who kept sending him back into the fray.

Rather than seek safety, he sought companionship and freedom from fear. He urged his friends to follow his lead, binding themselves one to another, even though that meant more vulnerability to loss, and seeking to rise above fear, even though that meant danger.

We cannot find safety in comfortable places, behind locked doors, in the faux serenity of settled questions, in the faux certainty of religion, in the predictability of "our kind," or in any painstaking assembly of wealth and privilege. If nothing else, death will find us. And if we make any effort to love, danger will find us, too.

QUESTION 18: "My stepdad is going through a terrible time in his life, and feels it's because God is punishing him for not serving him most of his life. How would you help a person to see that there may be other reasons for their hardships?"

> *[Jesus said,] "Or those eighteen who were killed when the tower of Siloam fell on them—do you think that they were worse offenders than all the others living in Jerusalem? No, I tell you; but unless you repent, you will all perish just as they did."* (Luke 13:4–5)

I meet with a friend. A situation is deteriorating. Frustration abounds. What can we do?

Not much, we conclude. We can only be patient, trust in God, and make sure our hearts are right.

In comparison with what other people suffer, my situation is merely a glitch. But even glitches can hurt and be confusing. Any suffering—from small accident to "terrible time" to wild disaster—exposes our vulnerability. As a popular prayer puts it, "Lord, the sea is so large, and my boat so small."

We ask "Why?" but don't probe too assiduously, for the abyss might be deeper than we imagine. We might see more about ourselves than we can accept, more about the brokenness of others, more about the chaotic nature of reality, or more about God. So our "Why?" is often more a whisper of vexation and helplessness than a determined inquiry.

One way out is to blame God—for being randomly cruel, or giving us what we deserve, or sending pain to make us stronger. Any of those works. Make God the cause of suffering, and avoid any serious inquiry into causation.

Take, for example, the eighteen killed at the "tower of Siloam." We know nothing about event or tower. Siloam referred to an aqueduct built in ancient times to carry water into the city. The aqueduct apparently ended in a pool (where Jesus healed a blind man) set between two walls. Perhaps one wall had a tower, and it collapsed.

Jesus used that tragedy in a call to repentance. The call is jarring, because it seems to suggest that God will cause towers to collapse, and worse, unless people repent. That straight-line causation—repent or suffer—leads inexorably to the reverse flow, as voiced by today's reader: If I suffer, it means I sinned.

Let's try another way. Let's assume Jesus knew his history, as well as his Scripture. The aqueduct known as Shiloah, or Siloam, was an example of human ingenuity. It helped to make the city of Jerusalem self-sufficient. Invaders destroyed it; the people repaired it. In its small way, Siloam was a symbol of Jerusalem's independence and grit, as well as its ambiguity as a city centered on temple and on commerce.

The water system made it possible for Jerusalem to meet basic needs but also encouraged the illusion of self-sufficiency, rewarding human ingenuity and yet losing touch with God's providence, ending in a pool of healing but stirring the bitter fruit of hubris along the way.

When we truly examine our suffering, that is what we encounter. Not just a question of God as cause or companion in suffering, but the complexity and ambiguity of being created able to build aqueducts and towers. Suffering, you see, is an invitation to self-examination, not along the single axis of blame, but in more disturbing questions such as, Am I suffering because I tried to build a tower in order to make myself superior to others and equal to God? Have I contributed to the very situation I find so frustrating?

The point isn't to fix the blame on God—or on self—but to look at the collapsing towers and to ask, Should I be building this tower? If so, then I ask God's help in my venture. If not, then I ask God's forgiveness and help in changing course.

QUESTION 19: "Why did you let my wife have that car accident that killed her? Don't you know how much of your good work she was doing and how much more she would do?"

[Jesus] told this parable: "A man had a fig tree planted in his vine-yard, and he came looking for fruit on it and found none." (Luke 13:6)

My latest automobile is a little sports car—well-used but sprightly— that I bought last summer when a family sedan began needing costly repairs.

I admit that safety wasn't uppermost in my mind when I took a test drive. I noticed speed, handling, and wind blowing through my hair. I saw immediately that SUVs and trucks towered ominously over me.

I was intrigued, therefore, by an article in the *New Yorker*, comparing my car with massive SUVs and declaring mine safer, because it gets into fewer accidents. But I don't place much stock in that logic. I have driven enough miles and seen enough vehicles suddenly collide to know that driving is inherently dangerous and there are no guarantees, no matter how alert and careful I try to be.

Other than avoidable foolishness like driving drunk or speeding, automobile accidents are the perfect metaphor for the randomness of suffering. Even when there is a discernible cause—weather, mechanical failure, another driver—the cause is usually beyond prevention. Some accidents just happen. Our lack of control can be maddening.

The question becomes: how important is it to think oneself in control? Can we tolerate a universe where control is an illusion? Can we accept randomness—not just the randomness of auto accidents, but the randomness of everything, from falling in love to a child's IQ to onset of cancer? Can we accept chaos, uncertainty, unpredictable consequences, the staggering likelihood that good decisions produce surprising results and good people suffer no less than bad people?

Many say, No. Such randomness is too threatening. They want control. Hence our tendency to name enemies and to scapegoat. (Bad things happen because some person or group causes them to happen.) Hence our obsession with sex. (Control over another person will make me feel better.) Hence our delight in the politics of blaming, as opposed to problem-solving. Hence our movement toward controllable environments like television, kitchens, and computers. Hence our rage when cable goes down.

Hence our creation of a God who has a plan, who causes all things to happen, who dispenses suffering in order to punish or to instruct. Hence our building of a church on the cause-and-effect legalism of Paul, rather than the parable-telling and noncontrolling of Jesus of Nazareth, for whom ministry was one random encounter after another.

Many would rather paint God a demon than live in a world where no one, not even God, is in control.

A reader lost his wife to a car accident. Many know the pain of such a loss. Many dread receiving that telephone call. Adding to the agony is a sense of unfairness, of worthiness going unrewarded, of a life well lived not being able to forestall suffering.

What sense, then, do we make of Jesus' parable of the fig tree? Was the accident victim being punished? Was her life a fruitless tree and she was being cut down? I imagine her husband shouting, "No! She was a good person!"

The parable, however, wasn't about the fig tree, but about the gardener. We want it to be about the tree, because its cause-and-effect preserves our fundamental need for control. But Jesus was describing a gardener—himself—who steps beyond worthiness and simply intercedes for bad and good alike. That isn't new behavior for God. Remember Abraham bargaining for Sodom? But it isn't entirely welcome, for we instinctively prefer a God of logical consequences, rather than compassion.

The gospel, however, is grounded in randomness. We need to embrace God as comforter and let go of God as controller.

QUESTION 20: "Why is there so much suffering? It seems so unfair."

[Jesus said: "So the owner] said to the gardener, 'See here! For three years I have come looking for fruit on this fig tree, and still I find none. Cut it down! Why should it be wasting the soil?'" (Luke 13:7)

Despite my efforts at reconciliation, an acquaintance lashes out at me. With smirking glee, he levels me and others with a verbal broadside that makes no distinctions and takes no prisoners.

I know this comes from inside his tormented soul. But still I ask, What was the point of my trying so hard? Why did I endure yesterday's abuse if today simply brings more?

This is a small incident compared with the vast suffering that can occur. Readers tell of loved ones dying, children committing suicide, marriages collapsing, jobs evaporating, and being left both angry and confused. Why, one asks, does life feel so "unjust and unfair"?

Suffering has that impact. To judge by your "roadside questions," suffering leads inexorably to feelings of confusion, self-doubt, anger at God, and betrayal, and from there to questions. Why is this happening? What did I do wrong? How could God do this or allow this?

I think asking such questions makes the pain more bearable. The raw agony of a chair left unoccupied is more than the normal soul can bear. We sense that pure emotion might drive us over the edge, or drive away the friends and family we count on for support, or render us temporarily unfit for the duties of life. So we cool our flame by asking unanswerable questions.

Our questions offer escape for those around us, too. Some of the harshest, least loving words ever spoken are the pastel phrases we utter to the suffering as we back away. "God must have wanted her more." "God has a plan." "God never sends us more than we can bear." "Just remember the good times." "You'll get over this." "Call me if you need anything."

Do we even hear the self-protective cruelty in such nonsense? The chair across the room is empty! That is the reality. That is the pain that starts, stalks, and stains the day. If you can't stay in the moment, within the toxic blast of my rage and agony, then take your platitudes elsewhere. Maybe I'll look you up when the pain subsides.

So let's hear the rage within the question, and let's look to God. We won't find pastel phrases or distancing answers. We will find Jesus bargaining with God.

God's rage had overflowed its banks. Despite millennia of loving-kindness, God's efforts at reconciliation had come up empty. Humanity was farther away than ever, killing at will, enslaving the weak, rejecting the stranger, wrapping itself in the flag of piety and politics, and turning God-things to shallow festival and meaningless argument. Even the gift of a Son—even the intimacy of Word made flesh—was leading nowhere. Three years of ministry, and all Jesus had was fools for disciples and pious prigs for enemies.

God's rage now stormed, "Cut it down!" No more of this barren tree!

Jesus intervened. He asked for one more year. A year in which he would give his life for the tree.

If there is any fairness in life, that is where we will find it. Not in an orderly march of events, not in outcomes that please and make sense, not in a creation where goodness pays off, accidents don't occur, wounds heal quickly, and friends are stalwarts.

We need to stop expecting such comforts. Our help isn't in a God who makes flawless systems, but in a God who stands at the same graves, who feels the same rage and pain, who knows despair, and yet who keeps trying. That is a companion fit for suffering.

QUESTION 21: "I would ask for emotional wholeness. Some part of my heart has died and I want it back."

[Jesus said: "The gardener] replied, 'Sir, let it alone for one more year, until I dig around it and put manure on it.'" (Luke 13:8)

Last fall, in a burst of optimism, my wife and I relocated the $12 shrubs that our builder had hastily planted in front of our new house just before handing us the keys. We bought four larger shrubs and envisioned a porch nestled in greenery.

Six months later, three of the four appear to have died. Poor product, poor planting, harsh winter? I don't know. If I were more of a gardener, I could verify their condition. As it is, I am only guessing. One solution, therefore, is to guess a little longer, let them remain in place for another season, perhaps add fertilizer, and make a decision next fall.

Task avoidance, of course, isn't the same as discernment, just as delaying consequences isn't the same as forgiveness.

A reader seeks "emotional wholeness." Her need is far more significant than a shrubbery problem, of course. But her statement—"Some

part of my heart has died"—makes me think of my wax myrtles. I think
they are dead, but I don't really know. They might be heartier than
I imagine. Spring warmth might work wonders. I don't want to give up
on them prematurely.

This is God's dilemma, too, as well as our own. When does one give
up on a fig tree? After one season, as in Mark 11, or after three? When
should God give up on Israel? After seeing Adam and Eve wearing fig
leaves as aprons? After seeing the Hebrews yearn for the fig trees of
Canaan but then abuse God's gift of a promised land? After Hebrew
exiles in Babylon won Jeremiah's praise as "good figs" worth preserving
but then relapsed into apostasy once they returned to Zion? When does
God's patience run out?

When does our own? Do we wait endlessly for a marriage to come to
life, for abuse to cease, for addiction to wither of its own accord, for
sadness to vanish, for a life partner to appear, for a painful childhood to
stop hurting?

Some of the suffering questions that readers asked refer to events
that happened long ago but still hurt. What is amazing is how fresh the
yearning for wholeness feels. Today's reader isn't alone in sensing death
but still hoping for life. And not hoping in the idle way that I hope my
shrubs aren't as dead as they seem, but real hope, a hope that enables
her to keep on living despite brokenness.

Such hope in the face of suffering seems deeply embedded in the
human soul. It is rare that we overtly give up. We seem to have integrated into our psyches, perhaps without knowing it, the belief of the
gardener in Jesus' parable, that if we just had one more season, and
maybe a little help, things would work out.

Perhaps Paul's greatest insight was that God has planted in each of
us what Paul calls a "spirit of sonship," a recognition of self as child of
God, which enables us to cry out, "Abba! Father!" In a visceral region
more real than creed, dogma, or religious affiliation, we simply know
that God exists, and we know God as good, source of life, healer of
broken hearts.

In asking for time, the gardener didn't set a timetable, like those
apocalyptic deadlines that sell books and populate mountainsides. The
gardener was saying, "Don't give up. Don't lose patience. There is always
hope."

Hope doesn't make the pain go away. But it does make today worth
living. And today and tomorrow are God's province. For God's dream
won't be thwarted. My shrubs might be dead, but in the serious realms
of life, hope endures.

QUESTION 22: "I would ask God about suicide. I have bipolar disorder and have attempted suicide once. I now have great resolve to accept responsibility for my illness and not to allow 'temporary despair' carry me into that intolerable abyss. Yet I do think about it when the pit envelops me."

[Jesus said: "The gardener said,] 'If it bears fruit next year, well and good; but if not, you can cut it down.'" (Luke 13:9)

I don't know why I didn't see the film *Elizabeth* when it debuted six years ago. But I am glad to watch the DVD tonight, for it helps to make sense of the day.

In the film starring Cate Blanchett as young Elizabeth ascending England's throne, director Shekhar Kapur took liberties with historical fact and seemed as much guided by Michael Corleone's torment in *The Godfather* as anything. But he captured an era's palace intrigues, brutal warfare, and, most especially, the violent arrogance of religious warfare, where believers stop at nothing to promote their slant on faith.

I got a slight taste of that capacity for violence today, as some readers of my weekly newspaper column pelted me with e-mail attacks ranging from name-calling ("You moron") to threats of eternal damnation. I am glad they don't live next door.

The direct line between religion and violence is staggering, as any study of history will show. In this sixth meditation on suffering, therefore, let's consider the suffering of God.

Much has been made recently about the suffering of Jesus in his final days, and rightly so. However over-the-top Mel Gibson's depiction of it might be, the passion is a central moment in the gospel drama. But it signifies something deeper than blood in the streets.

God has been suffering from the dawn of creation. Read Genesis 2–3, and hear God's agony as he discovers Adam and Eve hiding in shame. Read about the flood, when God's anger overflowed and then God repented. Read about the Hebrews' whining in the wilderness, David's betrayal, Solomon's vanity, the folly of weak kings—and hear God's suffering in the words of the prophets.

Many prefer to see God hovering serenely above the fray, observing the human condition but being little moved by it. But I believe the deeper scriptural theme is of a God who suffers, who experiences something similar to the mood swings and enveloping despair described by today's reader.

What does God do with such suffering? The Passion Narrative shows Jesus accepting humanity's brutality in order to save humanity. There is more, however.

A reader asks about suicide and voices her determination not to give in to "temporary despair." That is precisely the situation facing God.

People—God's beloved creation—are both strong and weak, blessed with capability and yet helpless before our passions, eager to love and yet quick to hate, yearning for freedom and yet satisfied with bondage, equally able to sing and to shout, to bless and to curse, to value life and to take life, to laugh and to rage. We visit our bipolarity on everyone and everything, and especially upon God.

How is God to respond? The flood, in retrospect, was like an act of suicide, and God vowed, "Never again" to such "temporary despair." What does that leave?

It leaves a gardener bargaining for time. "One more year," he says in Jesus' parable. But we know from the rest of Scripture that the year will end, and humanity's hope will lie in yet another reprieve. That is why the one-death-serves-all arithmetic of the passion isn't deep enough. God's response to suffering isn't to hold his fire, but to put down his weapon, to allow hope the victory.

How would God answer a question about suicide? I think God would say, "I know how you feel. But let's wait a minute, or a year, or as long as it takes for hope to return."

QUESTION 23: "I have just lost my beloved husband of 54 years to pancreatic cancer. My cry from the deepest depths of my heart would be, Lord Jesus, when I depart this world, will I see him again?"

[Jesus said,] "Then they will see 'the Son of Man coming in a cloud' with power and great glory." (Luke 21:27)

On the night before Thanksgiving Day, we prepare to "gather together to ask the Lord's blessing."

We will be seven this year: the five of our nuclear family, one girlfriend, and one father-in-law. We could be eight, if my wife's mother hadn't died twelve years ago. Her place will be empty. We could be twenty-three, if job mobility hadn't taken siblings so far from one another.

Every year it's a different count. Same menu, different faces, different stages of life. Romance brings new, death takes old, and growing up—college for two nieces, navy duty for a nephew, leaving home as adults for four sons—brings separation.

We can move chairs around, but rearranging the corners of our hearts isn't so easy. We are like those early pilgrims: making new lives far from home, unsure how to survive in a new and hard land, dependent on strangers, yearning to see God's bounty in landscapes that feel foreign, wondering how we got here, not knowing what lies ahead.

At our night-before dinner, we discuss a family recipe book that my wife wants to make for a nephew and his new bride. "What did Mom used to cook?" she asks. None of us can remember. It seems odd. We ate appreciatively at her table, but cannot remember what her meat loaf, "noodly stuff," or pot roast tasted like, or what else she served.

Those experiences, and memories we thought would last forever, have passed into God's hands. We are left vaguely enriched, vaguely depleted, never quite escaping the pilgrim's feeling of strangeness, wanting to name our children after ancestors they will never know, wanting to name new homes after places our people used to live—New Ipswich, New York, New Jersey, New Zealand, Berlin, Rome, Athens, Mexico, Moscow.

What does God do with our memories? Treasure them, surely, for they make us what we are, the beloved of God. Weep over the bitter, rejoice over the sweet, and always feel a kinship with us, for God's own memories are infinitely numerous, the empty places at God's table are beyond counting. God knows what we know, God feels what we feel.

Like grieving survivors who put words into a loved one's absent mouth in order to get their way, we are prone to make God small and mean: a vengeful judge, a narrow gate, a scorekeeper, a partisan in our little wars, a fastidious tyrant who smites and smolders in exactly the ways we would smite and smolder.

What we need to see is a mansion that has room for every one of us, a heart whose capacity for sadness and joy is beyond our comprehension, where a mother's pot roast lives as a token of steadfast love, where a husband of fifty-four years waits for his companion, where all that God loves and treasures will come to fulfillment.

On that day the Son of Man will lead a Thanksgiving Day parade of God's true "power and glory"—which is not the power to destroy or a glory that beckons only an elite, but the power to love and the glory of loving freely, without counting the cost.

At tables both meager and full, with empty places and new faces, where survival seems hard enough and abundance still a dream, we are bold to sing:

Even so, Lord, quickly come to thy final harvest home;
gather thou thy people in, free from sorrow, free from sin;
there, forever purified, in thy presence to abide;
come, with all thine angels come, raise the glorious harvest home.

QUESTION 24: "Why did God take my mom home to be with him when he did?"

Mary remained with [Elizabeth] about three months and then returned to her home. (Luke 1:56)

In a variant of "buyer's remorse," my wife and I wish we could stay home and listen to *A Prairie Home Companion.*

But our son wants to see a favorite teacher perform in her church's Christmas pageant. So off we go to share an evening with strangers.

This pageant turns out to be wonderful. Instead of children being cute, it is over 100 adult choristers and actors, teenagers and little kids energetically weaving together one family's alienation from God, the Christmas story, and the larger story of Jesus' life.

The family's issue is Dad. He works too hard, tells too many lies, and never comes home on time. People start to pray for him. He gets jolted out of his complacency by bad news on health and career, pours out his heart to a stranger, visits his pastor, and finds his way home to God and to his family.

You can see the ending coming, but that doesn't lessen its poignancy. For his story touches us all: the lies we tell in order to get by, our self-serving journeys, getting lost, hurting those who depend on us, forgetting where home is. I could do without the neat-as-a-bow theology— prayer works, the lost sheep comes home, his cancer diagnosis was erroneous, he gets promoted rather than dismissed, and his family shares a group hug. But the promise of home rings true.

The familiar Christmas music rings true, as well. Their overwrought renditions make me yearn for the simple cascading of sound that a friend provides for his congregation. But the invitation to "come and behold him" transcends staginess.

"That was really touching," says my twelve-year-old son. "I would like to do more at our church."

This is a season of "home." People decorate their homes. Grown-up children come home. Entire families endure congested airports and highways to go home. People yearn for homes they once had. People sense afresh the absence of those who made home happen.

I don't know that death occurs because God has called someone home. Just as God must wait for the sinner to yearn for home, so must God wait for our bodies to suffer more illness, accident, or warfare than they can bear. But I do believe that God makes a home for us, both here on this mortal coil and in eternity. Like the father in Jesus' parable, God scans the horizon for our return and rushes to greet us.

A reader asks, "Why?" The why of death's timing is beyond our understanding. But the why of God's "welcome home" has a clear answer: God loves. Surround that truth with overwrought music, sermons that are too long, and stories that are too simplistic, and the truth remains: God loves. Argue as we will over who deserves God's favor, and the truth remains: God loves.

Home is where we are loved without condition, without reservation, without our having to pay any price or earn any favor. At home, we know we are loved. At home, our lies are overcome by patience, and our failings are occasions for comfort. At home, we can dare to grow up, then dare to leave, then dare to return chastened, then yearn to return bearing partners and offspring. At home, lovers wait for us to come to our senses.

We might or might not attain such a home in this lifetime. I know I am extraordinarily blessed. But the promise of faith is that God prepares such a home for every one of us. As difficult as this life might be, as untimely as our homecomings might seem, God looks for us.

It is God who sang, "Joy to the world!" before we knew the tune.

Chapter 3

A Mother's Death

QUESTION 25: "What is eternal life?"

[John said,] "He will baptize you with the Holy Spirit and fire."
(Luke 3:16)

INDIANAPOLIS—My mother died yesterday after a long illness. The family is gathering.

She was born into the Roaring Twenties, came of age during the Great Depression, graduated from college into World War II, married midwar, started a family as the long war wound down, and raised that family through the vast sea changes of the postwar era.

She was a loving partner to a hometown boy she met in church. She supported him in building a business, in creating a happy home, and in stirring their children to intellectual curiosity, compassion, and open-mindedness. She had her own life, too, focused on volunteer work on behalf of such needy people as the mentally retarded.

Little of her was left when she died. Her zest and shy smile live on in her three children and seven grandchildren. Her mind lives on in their keen minds. Her love lives on in a husband who will be the first to admit that she made him a larger person.

What about the rest? What happens at death? I have no evidence to offer. But faith is never about evidence. Here is what I believe:

I believe that when she took her last breath, something passed to my father as he held her hand. A calmness, I think, that will carry him forward. Something passed to my sister, who stood nearby. A mantle, perhaps. Something passed to me when I heard of her death five minutes later. A perspective, I think, that some things matter more than others, and people matter most of all.

Some day, my father will pass his gift to me, and in time I will pass it to my three sons. They will be larger for it.

As for Mom herself, I believe that a door opened, and she walked on through, and there she was greeted by Jesus. I picture her walking resolutely, happily, peacefully. I picture him welcoming her, friend to friend.

Beyond that, I have no picture. That is okay with me. Death is for God, and eternity will come in due time.

"What is eternal life?" a reader asks. This is what I believe it is, at least in part. I suspect there is much more to be discovered some day. I feel no need to define it, to build a boundary around it, or to declare some people unsuitable for it. I know that I am not bereft about my mother's dying, because she was ready and unafraid, and because I believe God will remember God's own promises, not those fear-filled and often hate-filled words that some Christians proclaim as God's promises.

Over the past eighteen months, since Mom became ill, many of you have written me to share your concern. Many of you have been praying for her and for our family. I want you to know how grateful I am for your tender mercies. This is another dimension of eternal life, the way one person's suffering evokes compassion, and that compassion changes one and then others, and soon even people who don't know each other are connected by God in a circle of caring.

In this way, a woman once described as having a "soft voice and gentle tread" touched lives far beyond her small range of activity. She spent her entire life within a radius of one mile. And yet today, thousands feel what I felt the other night as, from 670 miles away, she gave me a final tap on my shoulder and said a mantle falls now to me.

This is fire, this is Holy Spirit, this is eternity—not some dread punishment or vengeful havoc, but a gentle tap on the shoulder, saying it is time to live even more fully.

QUESTION 26: "God, how do I cope with a culture that is the antithesis of you in almost every aspect?"

Now when all the people were baptized, and when Jesus also had been baptized and was praying, the heaven was opened, and the Holy Spirit descended upon him in bodily form like a dove. (Luke 3:21–22)

INDIANAPOLIS—When I drove north yesterday after my mother's death, I ran into snow in West Virginia. My white sports car was left a sludgy mess.

Today, after twenty-four hours of jousting with the funeral home, gasping at the price of a newspaper obituary ($300 a day for what ought to be free), sitting in my mother's chair at the breakfast table, selecting a burial site in the family plot, and going for a pensive walk with my sister, I decide it is time for Mike's Express Car Wash.

I choose the basic $7 package, which removes dirt and salt from the journey. This entails getting in line, following instructions, steering my left wheels onto a conveyor belt, putting the car in neutral, and taking my foot off the brake. After a deluge of suds and water, I am carried through powerful fans that rattle my convertible top but leave me dry for the journey onward.

Forget the tidy rituals of church baptism. Here at Mike's is the real thing.

We're dealing with dirt—the grime of a difficult journey. Not the theory of dirt, but the fact. Not a theology of sin, but observable consequences of driving hard. Not just dirt, but salt—"liquid salt," they call it, as if the state highway department were crying on its roads.

We're dealing with real cleansing and what it takes to get clean. Pulling off the road, allowing oneself to be led and carried, releasing the brake, enduring a noisy and aggressive process, being blown by strong wind.

I suspect the baptism of Jesus was more like this car wash than like the typical church baptism at a side altar. The early church declared Jesus forever free from sin. But the gospels actually say little about his first thirty years. It is just as likely that he lived a normal life and arrived at the Jordan the way my car and I arrived at Mike's: grimy from the journey, needing some strong cleansing. The point of his baptism wasn't what preceded it, but what followed.

A reader asks how he can cope with a culture that is antithetical to God. I wonder, first, how antithetical God and culture are. If God is viewed as residing at side altars and waiting for tidy rituals like Christian baptism, then the gap is wide. But maybe God is like Mike's Express Car Wash: always open for business, just pull off the road and let yourself be led. Maybe God, like Mike's, is in business because the journey is hard. The grime of life—cultural grime, family crisis grime, personal failings grime—isn't an offense against God, but is God's reason for being. Why send a messiah if people aren't in exile? Why be offended if the people whom Jesus came to save actually need saving?

I wonder, second, why the righteous need to portray Jesus as innocent and baptism as mild. Jesus knew too much of life to have been innocent. His compassion didn't come from a textbook, but from having tasted liquid salt. His personal rebirth led him immediately into the wilderness to be tested by Satan. His re-creating of the disciples was no less disruptive. Faith starts on the road, and baptism means a cleansing of roadway grime and a rekindling of courage for the journey.

After its bath at Mike's, my car sparkles. Will it stay that way? Only if I stop driving. For driving home after Mom's funeral will expose me to the dirt again. That is life. And that is where I will find God.

QUESTION 27: "Ahhhh . . . to ask my heart's desire at the 'roadside.' My Lord, please send me someone to love (and love me back). Your choice this time, dear Lord, not mine."

On the third day there was a marriage in Cana of Galilee, and the mother of Jesus was there. Jesus and his disciples had also been invited to the wedding. (John 2:1–2)

INDIANAPOLIS—I bring my camera but am so caught up in the golden glow of the moment that I forget to take pictures.

Three children, three children-in-law, six grandchildren, and two family friends bearing a feast—all gathered in my sister's kitchen, playing hearts and chess, watching pro football, chatting and laughing, all because a young man and woman chose to join their lives in the middle of a war.

That woman waits across town to be buried. The man sits contentedly as commotion swirls around him.

I marvel as cousins rekindle their bonds and challenge their parents to a game of charades. I marvel as spouses add their unique touch to family rituals. I marvel at the volume, intensity, joy, connection, and centeredness of this gathering. I marvel at how much can follow when God brings two people together.

Was it just the joining in 1943 that yielded all this? No, it was sixty years of effort, self-sacrifice, doubt, worry, hope, good fortune, good friends, and faith. No durable family happens just because a marriage occurs. It takes merging of lives, yielding of self-will, submission of self-interest, trusting in tomorrow—perhaps the hardest work we ever attempt.

Families are formed in the seemingly unremarkable rituals of evening meals, bedtime stories, games, trips, walks around the block, and letting go. Families are formed in those unnoticed moments when parents discuss their children and dream their own grown-up dreams. Families are formed when harsh words are spoken and resolved, when children disobey and are forgiven, when everyone fails in due season and is trusted with another chance, when new personalities are allowed to enter and the family to change. Families are formed when death occurs and life goes on.

I think we now realize that families take many shapes, only a few of which would qualify for the TV evangelist's description of "traditional." But the yearning for family tends to sound alike as each person gives voice to it. In fact, the yearning for family might be our strongest yearning, and all others—dreams of wealth, prowess, and fun—are substitutes for what we really want, namely, to be in close and loving relationship with a few other people.

If I could write the script for our times, I would urge two themes. One is that we all relax and let families take their own unique courses. Some, like the marriage at Cana, will follow the path of tradition: a man and a woman exchanging religious vows. Some, like the union of Joseph and Mary, will follow alternative stars. Some, like the friendship of Jesus and his male and female disciples, will chart other courses. There is no predicting what will happen when people allow love to reshape their lives. To insist on one way might sound righteous, but it isn't true to Scripture or to human nature, and it can be downright cruel.

Second, I would urge us to notice the love-starved. Many people feel unloved, unconnected, unknown, and therefore unworthy. Jesus formed circles and insisted they remain open. That insistence confused and angered many, because once we have found our belonging place, we often tend to close ranks and pull up the drawbridge, as if sharing the gifts would mean losing them.

But grace is more elastic than that. Tonight's glow began as two and now fills a large room. Every one of us was invited to the feast. Family isn't a treasure to be hoarded, but a dozen more invitations waiting to be issued.

QUESTION 28: "How can I find a way to make the parts of my life fit together, to make sense?"

When the wine gave out, the mother of Jesus said to him, "They have no wine." And Jesus said to her, "Woman, what concern is that to you and to me? My hour has not yet come." (John 2:3–4)

INDIANAPOLIS—I had thought ninety minutes would be too long for visitation prior to my mother's funeral. It turns out to be too short.

When service time comes, many are still waiting to speak to the family. They come from all parts of our lives: childhood friends, former and current neighbors, work associates, public television, Colonial Dames, Women's Club, Rotary, tennis, bridge, various churches and, most profoundly, this handsome church where my parents poured out their lives in service.

Partly this reflects eight decades lived in the same city. But it is far more than that. My mother knew how to form relationships. So does my father. Neighbors became friends. Club and work associates became friends. Fellow volunteers and parishioners became friends. Through openness and kindness, my parents reached across the chasm of anonymity and made friends.

As our family church went from the 1940s to the new millennium, into that diversity which threatens so many Episcopalians, my parents knew how to accept the new and, consequently, to become ever-new themselves. They knew how to embrace change and, consequently, to change themselves. It was never a cause, but a natural consequence of living openly and trustingly.

Many more go straight to the church and sit behind us. I am focused on caring for my father, so I don't see them. But I sense the welcome weight of their presence. Many in this assembly will continue to care for my father as family depart. I have no hesitation about leaving, because I trust this cloud of witness.

A smaller group gathers for lunch. Some are from that astonishing world called "family." Some are friends. I watch seven grandchildren share their table with two men whom none knew beforehand. Their conversation is lively.

At the cemetery, the gathering is smaller still. Just family and clergy. It feels, well, dead. Here among the dead we leave one who has died. We leave as quickly as possible, not because this place is morbid or death is off-putting, but because life is out there, where my mother taught us to live.

A reader asks how he can cause the parts of his life to "fit together" and "make sense." I doubt that he can. I don't think life works that way. Separate circles tend to remain separate circles. What he can do is be a friend in each circle. He can be the one who makes room, who accepts the stranger, who lets go of old attitudes, who allows change to occur, who rises above feeling threatened by diversity.

In a sense, we have to allow life to push us forward. We don't choose our neighbors, but we can choose to make friends with them. We don't choose our in-laws, but we can choose to love them. Some try to enforce sameness in their clubs and groups, but usually that effort fails and makes them bitter. Better, I think, to greet the new with a smile. Some try to control their worlds—"manage change," "maintain standards," "defend tradition"—but such control is delusional and frustrates God.

It's like Jesus and his mother at the wedding. He wasn't ready to move on to active ministry. He was still assembling disciples. But life was ready. As often happens in life, his mother pushed him onward. She saw the needs—a wedding's need for wine, and her son's need to get on with it.

Jesus had no control over the circles that awaited him. All he could do was be a friend and a lover in each one.

QUESTION 29: "Why are we often so lonely?"

[Jesus'] mother said to the servants, "Do whatever he tells you." . . . Jesus said to them, "Fill the jars with water." And they filled them up to the brim. (John 2:5, 7)

Before dawn, a niece returned to training camp for lightweight crew. Did anyone on her flight recognize signs of Wednesday's funeral? Did her teammates make room for her grief?

Later, my wife, three sons, and I started our two-car caravan south. We were quieter than usual, as we reflected on events since my mother's death and prepared ourselves for return to schools and offices.

Today my brother and his family return to the Northwest. After two long flights among strangers, they will rejoin a world that seems far away, perhaps disconnected. My sister will reclaim a house that was brimming with family life, then observe her first birthday without Mom.

Tonight my father will spend his first night alone.

I don't know which is loneliest: being home alone, being in a crowd alone, being among colleagues and classmates alone, or being within one's closest circle and still feeling alone.

I think lonely just is. I don't think loneliness is a sign of a life poorly lived, as if one should have made more friends or moved less often. I don't think loneliness is life's punishment for being too different, too passive, too assertive, too anything. I think loneliness is part of life.

As reflective beings, we observe life even as we live it. We see the crowd and ourselves in the crowd, and we feel the gap between self and other. When we speak, we observe the impact of our words. When we embrace, we sense the otherness of the one hugging back. We laugh or cry and wonder what others make of our emotions. We measure ourselves in comparison—that is, in separation.

Life crises push us more deeply into that separateness which already burdened us. Most people didn't understand us before, and they surely know nothing of us now. They stood apart when we felt able to connect, and they surely are distant now. Or so it seems.

We are like the jars that Jesus touched. Full or empty, but always separate, like those jars at Cana. Filled with water or wine, but always separate. Set among joy or sorrow, but always separate.

Once his mother goaded him to action, Jesus had two instructions. First was, "Fill the jars with water." Second was, "Now draw some out." Somewhere in the middle water became wine.

Life has a way of filling us up, sometimes with treasures and attributes deemed positive, sometimes with bitterness and grief. We probably have little control over what fills us. Jars, after all, are vessels being acted on by outside forces.

What God does is transform our contents and pour us out for others. Our sadness, for example, can build bridges to others. When our family processed to the front pew and sunlight broke through a leaden sky, flooding the nave with light, people didn't applaud us for deserving sunlight, but hugged the light to their own wounded hearts. Among the several hundred kind notes that readers have sent me are many that spoke of their own losses and grief. We don't attend funerals because we are morbid, but because there is living water being poured out.

I doubt that college friends took much notice of my niece's grief. But she is different now, pouring something new out of her life, and that wine will be tasted. However brusque and uninterested our classmates and colleagues seem on our return, God is drawing something new out of us, and that wine will be tasted.

Yes, life is inherently lonely, and yet God transforms even our most sour separateness into something sweet. We just need to let our jars be filled or emptied, as life and God desire.

Chapter 4

Purpose

QUESTION 30: "What shall I now do with my life?"

[Jesus] told them a parable: "Look at the fig tree and all the trees; as soon as they sprout leaves you can see for yourselves and know that summer is already near." (Luke 21:29–30)

Morning brings cloudy skies, balmy air, and short sleeves on the golf course. By noon, rain is falling, and golf is over. By evening, cold air is blowing in, signaling autumn's transition to winter.

Morning brings a full house to the breakfast table, while I preside at the griddle. Two leave after dinner, a third leaves today, and a fourth on Monday. We will be three again.

Horizons vary. My twelve-year-old son wonders if his brothers have to leave today. Older sons are looking farther ahead at career choices and next homes. I take a peek at next week's work schedule, make travel plans to visit my hometown, and contemplate next spring's lawn plans. My wife does a research paper.

We all keep time by the same calendar and dodge the same rain, but we see different signs. I stand on a broad porch and see a landscaping project. My sons see a road leading elsewhere. My father-in-law sees a hill that becomes difficult to climb. My wife sees a need for flowers. Same view, different responses.

Shopping malls opened at 6 A.M. today. For some, that signals the start of something important. For me, it means commerce's annual encroachment on the holy and fragile.

It is one thing, as Jesus said, to see the fig tree sprouting leaves and to know that "summer is already near." It is another to gauge a unique response to that changing season. For horizons vary, and the same turning of the calendar stirs unique feelings in each of us.

One of religion's immature expressions is to declare a single way, a single path, a single belief, a single interpretation, a single ethic, a single correctness. Such triumphalism makes for punchy preaching, but it flies in the face of reality, and it wounds the many to please the few. Those whose lifestyles are portrayed as God's ideal feel warmly affirmed, and they demand more such preaching and condemn other viewpoints. But other people feel judged and diminished; they hear the lie in such proclamation and turn away.

"What shall I do now?" asks a reader. Take your own reading of the seasons, I say. It isn't enough to know that this is, say, the autumn of your years. What does autumn mean to you? Is it a time for planting or harvesting? The ads say your age means retirement, but that's just advertising for retirement planning services. It means nothing. The marketplace has you pegged, but that's just statistical probabilities, not life. Just because the stores open at 6 A.M. doesn't mean you have to stand in line.

Some believe God has a plan for your life. I don't believe that myself. I believe God will watch with interest as you make your own decisions, and will provide sustenance and love whatever you choose. That is more freedom and responsibility than many people want. But I believe it is reality.

So it's back to you: what do you want to do? Looking out over the landscape, do you feel an urge to plant grass, to take a walk, or to go back inside for a nap? We gauge, you see, not only the season out there, but also the season inside. At any given moment, we walk a line between what is possible and not possible, what is desirable and not desirable, between other people's needs and our own, between the timely and the untimely, between the deep and the shallow, between the decent and the expedient.

Forget the "shoulds" that other people would impose on you. They are just trying to make their worlds feel safer. Your seasons are different from theirs.

QUESTION 31: "How can I serve you?"

During the high priesthood of Annas and Caiaphas, the word of God came to John son of Zechariah in the wilderness. (Luke 3:2)

Being warned of weekend mobs, my wife and I slip away midafternoon to make our first visit to a new upscale food, coffee, and gift shop that will put every competitor out of business.

We endure a traffic jam caused by the highway department's bizarre decision to repair the area's busiest road during Christmas shopping season.

The store is a delight. Abundance everywhere. More types of coffee, tea, and cheese than I knew existed. Vast but tasteful displays of gourmet foods, cooking ware, and wines. Plentiful staff looking for ways to help. Ample checkout lanes.

I shouldn't be surprised. This is a university town, after all, where everything is presumed to work. No shabby corners allowed.

So why not just relax and let it happen? Why notice the traffic jam? Why question the store's social engineering? Why mutter "of course, what else would you expect in this precious college town?"

Part of me doesn't want to be seduced by retailing genius. But more than that, perfection makes me nervous. Even though I appreciate abundance and planning, the store reminds me of a new housing development where every house is ideal, alike, and isolated.

When we build a wall between the wilderness and ourselves, what happens on our side of the wall? For wilderness is where meaning is found. From the biblical epic to the struggles of emerging science, from the founding of nations to the early years of a family, wilderness is where true values are formed, people draw close for survival, food is shared, and small thanksgivings celebrated, where leaders have vision and people discover unexpected fortitude in themselves and grace in others.

I wonder how many of us shop in perfected stores, retrieve children from flawless schools, stop by well-organized soccer leagues, drive home in spiffy German cars to large homes with high-tech kitchens and entertainment centers, and then yearn for another place where we share bedrooms, play football in the street, fix up old cars, play people-centered games, weigh less, and do our cooking in hardware-store skillets.

It isn't that things were better back then—the 1950s being vastly overrated—but that something better exists over there, on the other side of the wall, where the issue is survival, not low prices every day.

We have closed off the wilderness, you see, and compartmentalized pain and aging as mistakes in body-chemistry management, sacrifice as unnecessary, values as derived from self, comfort as our entitlement, and strangers and ideas as dangerous.

A reader asks, "How can I serve God?" The first step, I think, is to do what John the Baptist did, namely, go into the wilderness. Leave behind the settled world of political order and established religion, and go into that wild place where the word of God can be heard.

We tend to look back at the New Testament era as a sad and depleted time just waiting for a church to be formed. In fact, it was a time of order and predictability, where most had made their peace with Roman oppression and only zealots imagined something else. Religion had become an effete acting out of small rituals, where people listened for familiar words and resented anything new.

It was a time, in other words, much like our own.

To hear the word of God, John the Baptist couldn't join his father Zechariah in ritual duty at the temple. He needed to leave Jerusalem and venture into the desert. That is what Jesus did, too.

We will serve God back here, for this is where lost souls are dying, but until we dare the wilderness and hear what God says beyond comfort and order, we will have nothing to offer but lawn-maintenance tips and arguments over privilege and style.

QUESTION 32: "Dear God, what do you want me to do for you?"

And the crowds asked [John], "What then should we do?" In reply he said to them, "Whoever has two coats must share with anyone who has none; and whoever has food must do likewise." (Luke 3:10–11)

I have more conversations today about our company's new 401(k) retirement plan, and about investment strategies in a volatile economy, how to obtain sound financial advice, and how to prepare for a retirement that isn't as far off as it once seemed.

I don't consider myself gifted in these areas, but year-end approaches and decisions for next year must be made now.

Year-end brings to my plate management decisions at work—salaries, benefits, next year's budget—and spending plans at home. "What should we do?" is a question ruling many lives.

In my pastoral days, I found year-end stressful. Church budgeting, personnel evaluations, and leadership elections inevitably meant conflict. People had different visions for what the church ought to be doing, how well it was currently performing, who was to blame for shortfalls, and how to use elections to pursue doctrinal or political agendas.

Meantime, we had Christmas bearing down on us. Worship to prepare, frazzled musicians to support, a surge in pastoral distress, needs at home, and most disconcerting, the phenomenal disconnect between the Advent/Christmas message and year-end frenzy.

Hope in God's providence collided with a human call to "realistic" planning. God's promise of mercy—that is, not giving us what we deserve—collided with worldly practices of accountability, such as performance reviews. A message of softness and submission fell onto the hard soil of politicking. Cheerfulness grounded in being loved was drowned out by our manic chasing of comforts and escapes.

It's easy to blame merchants for starting too early, and schlock culture for turning grand music into irritating noise. It's easy to blame the calendar for requiring sound business decisions at our most emotionally vulnerable time of year. It's easy to throw in the towel and to want it all: spend on gifts as if next year wasn't coming, and then cycle into remorse. Or hire an extra trumpeter for Christmas Eve, and then criticize the music minister for going over budget. Or press the pastor on performance and salary, and then expect 14-hour workdays, glad sacrifice of family time for pastoral needs, and a sweet sermon on Christmas Eve.

But that blaming would miss the point. Christmas was moved from spring to December specifically to conflict with a pagan winter-darkness festival. The Advent gospels are intended to call common conceptions of time and values into question. John's answer to the crowds is deliberately contrary to human nature. The birth-cry of Jesus and the angel-cry of peace appeared amid noise, warfare, oppression, and self-serving, and they forced the point: which matters more?

Our year-end stress isn't an accident of timing. It is a sign that we haven't yet heard God's answer to the reader's question, "What do you want me to do for you?" We don't need to move budget planning to a less combustible season. This is precisely when we should think about money and what it means to us. This is precisely when we should get power needs, control needs, and comfort needs into godly perspective. This is precisely when we should hold elections, and if we elect angry people for narrow self-serving reasons, we need to see the contrast between them and the shepherds who came to Jesus.

John's answer was clear: Be generous, be fair, be honest. Mary's answer was clear: Let your soul magnify the Lord. Joseph's answer was clear: Be steadfast for God even as events get confusing. Jesus' answer was clear: Love God, and love your neighbor.

There is no mystery about what God wants. The mystery is why we think we can have it all and not need to decide between God and mammon, between blessing and curse, between life and death.

QUESTION 33: "Jesus, how can I be sure of the path you want me to take and how do I know that the things being taught to me are really your will and not the will of man?"

Mary said, "My soul magnifies the Lord, and my spirit rejoices in God my Savior, for he has looked with favor on the lowliness of his servant." (Luke 1:46–48)

I turn on the radio and find myself midstream in choral works for the Christmas season.

A little Bach, a little Renaissance, not following a theological theme, but tapping memories of high school choruses, community choirs, and church services accompanying Christmas past.

The morning concert ends with "Hallelujah!" from Handel's *Messiah*. It is out of place, of course, because "Hallelujah!" ends the Easter section of *Messiah* and not the Christmas section. But the chorus that Handel composed in a single night of wild inspiration has become a shout of joy unrelated to church calendar.

That shout serves our need for jubilation, just as Christmas has come to serve our need for warmth, family, connection, hope. Strip away the commercialism, and you have moms baking cookies with kids, or memories of such baking, or a yearning for such a moment, or a less specific sense that year-end budgeting isn't all that life is about. In fact, the more anonymous and isolating that modern life becomes, the more we want from Christmas.

So church choirs set aside theological niceties and burst forth in "Hallelujah!" And it works. No one listens to the words of such a chorus. They hear joy, not Handel's tortured rendering of the nonpoetic word "omnipotent."

The question is what serves. It's the same question that walks alongside me all day, as I meet with colleagues and interact with family: what serves? Among the many choices open to me—kindness or cruelty, listening or talking, self or other, candor or deceit, self-awareness or delusion, open or closed, forward or backward, self-revelation or self-protection, giving or taking, helping or hindering, sacrifice or power—what is the servant's path?

The servant's path isn't easy to identify. Sometimes the hard word of truth helps, sometimes it simply hurts. An apology can be timely or premature, praise heartfelt or empty. Preserving authority is different from preserving power. Allowing someone to fail can be kindness or abandonment. It gets confusing. Hard-and-fast rules tend to be meaningless.

In the revisionist hands of the early church, Mary became a marble icon lifted beyond the human realm. But Luke knew her as something earthier—a gutsy woman, a leader among the apostles, elated by birth and saddened by suffering, able to stand by the cross when others fled. How did she attain such nobility? By the path of "lowliness" and servanthood.

Who knows whether or not the fourteen-year-old girl ever sang Hannah's song from 1 Samuel, or consciously made the intriguing theological connections between Hannah's son Samuel and her own son Jesus? The point about Mary is always that she said Yes to God and Yes to the new life that God would create in her.

It is that Yes to God and Yes to new life which mark the servant's path. We can bluster all we want about the correctness of our doctrine, the infallibility of our Scriptures, the absolute virtue of our rejections and divisions. But people don't listen to our words. They listen more deeply for what lies within, for the "servant's heart," as a friend puts it. I suspect God lost interest in our words long ago. We talk too easily about matters too wrenching for words.

How can today's reader know the right path? Look for lowliness and servanthood, not majesty and power. What builds up the other? What nurtures life? What allows God's radically new future to break in? What says Yes to the unknown? What will sing "Hallelujah!" in or out of season?

QUESTION 34: "What would you have me say, Lord? What would you have me do? What would you have me be? Show me the way to show my children your gifts."

Joseph got up, took the child and his mother, and went to the land of Israel. (Matthew 2:21)

My twelve-year-old son pulls out his questions and blank sheets of paper, and begins to interview me about my experiences in sixth grade.

What was school like? What did I study? Did we have cliques? Did people get into trouble? What were my favorite activities outside class? What did I do during summer vacation?

The questions are about me, and that will be his parallel: how the me of sixth grade relates to the him of sixth grade. But as I answer, I am aware of an active cultural context that was shaping me at a time when I wasn't aware of being shaped. I remember the music, safe neighborhoods, at-home moms, outdoor adventures, reading constantly, playing cards, shooting hoops, summer camp, rolled-up Levis.

I pull out a photo album to show him my family context: our family of four, the arrival of my baby brother making five, walking to my grandparents' house, the sparkle in my mother's eyes beside the Christmas tree, and the zest in my father's as he took us for a spin in his new Morris Minor convertible.

This is a school assignment, and his curiosity has limits. Some day he will explore the photo album. He will see the preadolescent uncertainty in my eyes and understand his own. He will see children looking serious about play and accept his own urgency. He will see the delight, questions, and wonder in my parents' eyes and sense that his parents are also on a journey.

Much he won't see. He won't see what it took for neighborhood friendships to happen, or church choir, or school events, or presents under the Christmas tree. He won't see my father driving off to work every morning and my mother balancing the books late at night.

But he will know that my life didn't just appear. It came from somewhere and grew slowly over time. I was carried on other shoulders. Like Joseph leading his family back to Israel, my parents made choices and took actions that made me who I am.

My son's last question is similar to that asked by today's reader: What would I say to sixth graders today? I don't hesitate. "Turn off your televisions," I would say. "Read more, work hard, try for good grades." In other words, make good choices, and take your life and mind seriously.

And know that some day you will make choices for others. Start now to get enough love into your heart, wisdom into your mind, and compassion into your soul for those to be good choices.

What would God have this reader say and do and be? Moses put it this way to the Hebrews: "Choose life." Whether that means turning off television or working on your marriage, choose life. Whether that means giving a child room to play safely or tending the sparkle in your own eyes, choose life.

We cannot live through our children, but we are obliged to make choices that enable them to live. We must see the dangers and protect them. We must see their yearning and dig deep in our hearts for love. We must stay awake so that they can sleep, and balance the books so that they can read *Harry Potter*, and pray aloud so that they can believe, and seek goodness in ourselves so that they can be good.

Someone gave that to us, as Joseph and Mary gave it to Jesus. At a time when they were young and confused, they gave life to their boy. He rarely talked of them, as our children rarely talk of us. But their choices counted. So do ours.

QUESTION 35: "How can my husband and I best live our remaining years so that we do not waste any time in the pursuit of unimportant things? I am 57, my husband is 59."

The people were filled with expectation. (Luke 3:15)

My warm-up shots today are encouraging. But even if they weren't, I would stand on the 1st tee expecting today to be better.

My first shot is strong and my second weak. It is the first, not the second, that lives in memory as I prepare for my third.

Over the next hours, my golfing performance ranges between delightful and desultory. Every good shot brings a smile of recognition—yes, I can do that—not a gasp of surprise. Even after finishing poorly, I find good reason to think ahead to our next outing.

Golf, in other words, doesn't make sense. The game itself is largely absurd, and the expectations it encourages unrealistic. Anyone who needs rational justification for action and who views tomorrow only through the lens of yesterday should stay away from the links. Too many dreamers out there. Too many men and women who select a club, stand before a ball, ignore the "cold hard facts" of what they won't be able to do, and swing eagerly, fully expecting a perfect shot, never being so discouraged by actuality that they stop believing.

Luke says that at the time Jesus made his appearance, the people of Israel "were filled with expectation." They believed a messiah was coming, and they wondered specifically whether John the Baptist was that messiah. Behind that specific question lay a larger expectation—hope, dream, belief—that tomorrow wasn't determined by yesterday.

Like our own stories, Israel's story had two components: actual events and possibilities. By any rational estimation, Israel's history was a grim and discouraging account. Eden led inexorably to flood. Abram's obedience led to Joseph's bondage. Liberation from bondage led to hardship. They claimed the promise of Canaan but immediately began to squander that promise. David forged a kingdom but betrayed God in his lust for Bathsheba. The united kingdom fractured, the weakened were overrun by stronger enemies and led into captivity. Their return from exile produced little more than an effete legalism and, by Jesus' time, a religious establishment focused on privilege.

And yet they never stopped believing it could be better. God saw dry land even as waters covered the earth. In Sinai God walked ahead of them, not behind them keeping score of their failings. God saw them as a "beacon to the nations" even when they were a small and self-serving tribe. God wept with them, even though they deserved exile. God saw a highway home to Zion where they could see only desert. God saw a branch of Jesse still to come, even though the original branch (David) had disappointed. After thirty-one years of marriage, a woman asks about the years that remain. She has her scrapbooks, no doubt, filled with pictures of yesterday. Unless she and her partner are superhuman, she also has corners of regret, memories of harsh words and disappointments, and long hours (years? decades?) of "unimportant things." No one gets to fifty-seven without having suffered and fallen short.

But listen to her question. Like the people of Israel and every golfer I know, she is "filled with expectation." How can they "best live (their) remaining years?" How can they make the time count? How can they avoid getting trapped in "unimportant things"?

The answer of faith—and of golf, for that matter—is this: treasure the expectation. Be filled with it. No matter what has gone before, believe that dry land can appear and exiles can end. John the Baptist might not be the one, and today might not be the day. But better does exist, and by the grace of God, better does come.

Why? Not because history is our guide, but because God is our guide.

QUESTION 36: "I am trying to grow an Internet business, and it has been very challenging. My question for Jesus would be, 'Is this what you want me to do?'"

When [Jesus] came to Nazareth, where he had been brought up, he went to the synagogue on the sabbath day, as was his custom. He stood up to read. (Luke 4:16)

As an entrepreneur, I know three things.

First, we must always reinvent the wheel. I know that is heresy to some, but failure to reinvent will doom the venture. Reality is too dynamic for settled ways to remain lively for long. So, by the way, is God.

Second, reinvention will always engender conflict. The fearful will protest. Those with no meaningful stake in reinvention will see aggravation, not opportunity. Competing visions will emerge. Failure will occur, and some will pounce on failure. Systems—corporate, family, church—are inherently resistant to change.

Third, self-doubt will occur—and ought to occur. Reinvention requires constant assessment of motivation, personality, direction, structure, systems, vision. The primary obstacle to reinvention tends to be oneself.

I am not at all surprised that a reader who is starting a new business is also asking whether he has chosen the right course. He would be a fool not to question his destination and plan for getting there. Asking questions is a sign of wisdom, not weakness.

When we write the history of successful ventures, we tend to see logical progress toward a worthwhile goal. We don't pay enough attention to fits and starts along the way, agonizing reassessments, missteps, inadequacies that had to be overcome, and the way destinations tend to change, until finally one arrives at a surprise.

I don't think we will ever understand Jesus or build a church worthy of his name until we recognize that he started one place and ended another. His life wasn't a seamless progression from stable to Calvary to glory. He changed course more than once, as his understanding grew and as reality intruded. In changing direction, he behaved like an entrepreneur: constantly assessing, taking risks, learning from failure, doubting himself, empowering others, and eventually reaching a place that was a long way from genial teaching within tradition.

Jesus figured it out along the way. Instead of laying all of his words on a table, like dishes at a church supper, and selecting a taste from here and a taste from there and calling it a meal, we need to examine crossroads when reinvention became essential.

That means examining discovery moments like teaching in his childhood synagogue, his encounter with the woman at the well, his disturbing dialogue with Peter, the transfiguration, and his agony in Gethsemane. Jesus was reinventing himself even as he died.

In my opinion, we must stop clinging to precedent and seamless hero stories. The life of Jesus was a messy journey, not a carefully constructed epic poem. He lived the way we live: one day at a time, one mistake at a time, one fresh discovery at a time. His hallmark wasn't consistency, but submission.

It is tragic that Christians have had so little stomach for discovery and change. We have tended to stifle the entrepreneurial spirit. We look backward when we should look forward. We fight over old words when we should listen for fresh words. We emulate the ancient when we should engage with today's reality.

To prevent change, we ignore certain needs, because seeing them would require reinvention. We marginalize certain people, because accepting them would require self-doubt. We make our fellowships shallow and safe, because depth would engender conflict and accelerate change.

Most vexing is that we have worn ourselves out on changes like liturgical renewal and reallocation of power, which were significant but not as deep as we needed to go. Now the world desperately needs us to go deeper, but we are too fragmented and exhausted to undertake the hard work of examining purposes and practices, which would be required before we could make a difference.

QUESTION 37: "How do I know I am 'called' to serve God in his church and community?"

[Jesus read from Isaiah:] "to proclaim the year of the Lord's favor." (Luke 4:19)

I inform a business partner that we have decided not to pursue a particular job, because it seems outside our current business model.

We keep on talking. My charge in our firm is to imagine the future, to scout out opportunities. This means listening to the marketplace, seeing unmet needs, forming alliances, dreaming while others handle the day-to-day.

As we talk, glimpses from this conversation join hands with other observations, and suddenly a "call" emerges. An entire scenario comes into view. I can imagine every step of it. I know from experience that actuality will reshape this vision many times. But I am intrigued at how a complete story can come to mind before the first sentence is written.

Not everyone thinks this way, of course. It was liberating and chastening to learn years ago, while doing the Myers-Briggs Personality Type Indicator, that others approach ideas and decisions quite differently.

A reader asks how she can verify being called to serve God. I take it that she is on some ordination track, where this question tends to be asked regularly. But the question should be asked by all Christians who want to serve.

Any call requires one to see what others aren't seeing. A teacher must imagine a student's moving from not knowing to knowing. A lawyer must imagine a problem's getting resolved. A salesperson must imagine a sale's being made. Sometimes that seeing is welcome; often it is unwelcome.

Jesus had a clear vision of his people. He saw them as lost, as having returned from exile but finding themselves still oppressed, still captive, still blind. His good news responded to ailments they weren't yet seeing.

Two things had to happen. First, they had to hear and respond to his vision of them. They did so, and they hated it. Second, Jesus had to let go of his vision, allowing reality and God to reshape it. That process commenced immediately and reached its conclusion in Gethsemane. It was a difficult journey for him to live—and difficult for us to understand, because it is a trajectory, not isolated sayings and events.

A testing of call, therefore, is hard work. Instead of asking a prospective ordinand or Sunday school teacher to explain why they want this job, we should ask: How do you see us? What vision do you have that we don't yet see? If your ministry succeeded, what would be different in this troubled world?

We tend to view candidates for church leadership as caretakers. We encourage them to think small, to promise us they won't change anything. We imply that their role is to protect some sacred flame that is already burning the way it ought to burn. Honesty, we hint, can be dangerous, vision can imperil their chance of approval, thinking outside the box is a no-no.

But think about it. Why would we want a teacher who cannot imagine a child needing to grow and being capable of growing? Why would we want a pastor who didn't see us as needing care? Why would we entrust our institutions to people who cannot imagine a future that is different from what we know?

Verifying a call, it seems to me, starts in seeing what there is to see, as Jesus did, and imagining a future. Then comes a question critical, and often conflict laden. What do you see in us? What do we see in you? How do we respond to what you see? How do you deal with our response?

We might as well acknowledge the conflict right up front, because that conflict between today and tomorrow, between my vision and your vision, is what will usher in the "year of the Lord's favor," or stifle it.

QUESTION 38: "I would shout at Jesus, 'What am I missing? Where are you present that I do not feel or see?' I would like to feel the calm 24-7."

[Jesus] passed through the midst of them and went on his way. (Luke 4:30)

My son goes to "Magic Night" at our neighborhood club. When they started these Friday "game nights" last fall, nearly twenty kids came. Tonight it is four.

Nothing stands still.

Today I resume the adventure of planning for retirement. I started three times before, but circumstances changed. With retirement years away but closer, it is time to start again.

Nothing stands still.

Moving on is one of life's great survival skills. Fall o
on. Lose a treasure? Move on. Fail at something? Mo'
from life? Move on.

It is more than a survival skill. Moving on is essential tu ,
emotional, and spiritual health. Too often we get stuck—stuck in old
ideas, stuck in harmful situations, stuck in inherited prejudices, stuck in
pain, stuck in faded dreams. We find ourselves paralyzed or imprisoned
by ourselves, by other people, by situations beyond our control. To the
extent possible, it is time to move on.

Moving on doesn't necessarily mean abandoning one's life or jetti-
soning other people. The answer to a troubled relationship isn't necessarily to pack a bag. More likely, it means moving on from whatever
self-defeating behavior or stored-up resentment has soured the bond.
Moving on might mean joining hands and stepping onward together.
But standing still isn't an option.

Religion has the hardest time moving on. Our current battles over
homosexuality strike me as just the latest outbreak of self-imprisonment
in fear of change. Over the centuries, Christianity's most basic instinct
has been to resist moving on, every time quoting Scripture to justify
resistance, every time being prodded onward by reality and eventually
seeing reality, only to have reality change again.

Some battles might be larger than others. Slavery was larger than new
hymns. Scientific discoveries were larger than which altar candle should
be lighted first. A fresh understanding of women was larger than
whether a downtown church should remain downtown.

But our instinctual response has tended to be the same. Bluster
against change agents, castigate modern culture, quote Scripture, draw
lines in the sand, take votes, reject votes, pack a bag, deny reality, ride the
ship down, wonder who's to blame.

A reader asks what she is missing and where Jesus is present. The
answer, I believe, is that Jesus is moving on. Rather than remain in
Nazareth and argue with his townsfolk, he "passed through the midst of
them and went on his way." Rather than engage in dueling Scriptures
and dueling traditions, he said what he had to say and moved on.

We cannot find a shrine where time stands still and ultimate truth is
always manifest and always the same. We cannot perfect an argument
and then stop wondering. We cannot assume that ancient sources comprehend today or tomorrow. There is no scholarship that will guarantee
safe harbor. There is no compilation of telling Scriptures that will answer
all questions or even the next variant of an old question.

Where will Jesus be found? In the present, not in the past. Moving on to someplace new—a new land, a new day in the familiar land, alongside a self straining to be new. Moving on to someplace else—not the tried and true, but onward, moving toward a promise, dreaming of wholeness in the midst of brokenness and life in the midst of death.

Will that be a place of perpetual "calm"? Almost certainly not. Peaceful, perhaps, but not the standing-still, don't-bother-me stasis that we often identify as peace. If you would seek Jesus, hear the angel at the tomb: "He is not here." He has moved on. So must we.

QUESTION 39: "How can I find a way to make the parts of my life fit together, to make sense?"

When Simon Peter saw [the full nets], he fell down at Jesus' knees, saying, "Go away from me, Lord, for I am a sinful man!" For he and all who were with him were amazed at the catch of fish that they had taken. (Luke 5:8–9)

LOUISVILLE, KENTUCKY—I walk through an airport that is like all airports: a construction site strewn with cones, temporary signs, and yellow tape.

My host tells me the entire airport is being redone. What they built a dozen years ago has become inadequate.

Before heading to a retreat center, we visit his church. It is a lovely example of contemporary architecture and has served this large congregation well. It was built as a finished product, not a work in progress. Its walls, windows, pews, and dramatic roofline connote permanence, the studied output of a fine architect.

All around this lively city, change is in the air, as economic opportunities and people's lives change. Even Hillerich & Bradsby, a 120-year-old company, has a handsome new building for that ancient craft of making Louisville Slugger baseball bats.

But this church, like most, resembles an unchanging rock, the same today as yesterday. Some find its space inflexible and confining, an obstacle to moving forward. Some guard that changelessness as a high calling—or, others believe, as an excuse not to change anything.

In a nearby suburb, a cleric tells an Episcopal study group that they may no longer read whatever they want. To ensure doctrinal discipline, clergy must approve their reading list and supervise their discussions. Group members are aghast. Where did this thought control come from?

My host relates a warning from a Southern Baptist friend, who saw fundamentalist ideologues seize Louisville's once-excellent Baptist seminary and turn it to rigid mediocrity. The strategy that ideologues used to take over the Southern Baptist Convention, he says, is exactly the strategy being used by fundamentalists to take over the Episcopal Church.

I wince at talk of conspiracies. But the Southern Baptist veteran warned his Episcopalian friends, "Don't be so naive. They have a plan." Maybe so. They certainly are relentless. Conspiracy or no, we are caught up in a wrenching tension between change and stability, between freedom and discipline, between diversity and uniformity.

Churches aren't alone in this tension. Airports, school boards, political systems, and universities feel it, too. But the church is uniquely ill equipped to respond. For we inherit buildings that seem too perfect to change, doctrines and creeds that we have promoted as absolute, and systems—leadership structures, educational norms, pastoral expectations, ways of interacting—that we treat as finished products.

Simon told Jesus to go away, because the suddenly full nets violated his worldview. In the same way, new members threaten a congregation's self-understanding. A new pastor threatens established ways. Growth threatens architectural integrity. New ideas threaten doctrine. New cries for help threaten everything the church holds dear.

The question before us is the question a reader raises: how to take these parts and fit them together in a way that makes sense.

Whatever our enterprise—a personal life or a corporate venture—we can't pretend that change isn't occurring, or that everything is perfect the way it is, or that wisdom lies in "Just say No." Mindless resistance leaves us more fragmented and more vulnerable to the darkness.

We need integrity, functional systems, wholeness, sense, and purpose. But we won't find them by turning churches into shrines, or by damning the new and free, or by circling the wagons in bitter conspiracies to stop modernity, or by doing the same old things in the same old way.

For a church, that means dreaming beyond the beautiful walls. For a person it means the same. It means rebuilding, renovating, re-creating, allowing God to fill our nets in new ways.

QUESTION 40: "What will God have to say to me when we meet face to face?"

[Jesus] looked up at his disciples and said: "Blessed are you who are poor, for yours is the kingdom of God. Blessed are you who are

hungry now, for you will be filled. Blessed are you who weep now, for you will laugh." (Luke 6:20–21)

My wife and I walk down the dingy, battered hallways of our youngest son's school—sights I don't see when I drop him off each morning. How has public education come to this?

We sit with four teachers to discuss our son's academic performance and deportment. They have keen minds and big hearts. Our son is a person to them, not a task. In view of abysmal pay and the inane burden of politicians' tests, how do they remain committed?

In our conference, I listen for character and curiosity. In what they see of him outside the family bubble, is my son growing as a person, as a leader, as a citizen? Is he living into his capabilities?

Good grades are a measure, but always on a sliding scale determined by giftedness and never an absolute in themselves. Good behavior is a plus, but only if chosen freely. The foundation he lays now won't be a flawless report card, but strong character and a curious mind.

The same will be true throughout his life. The world will measure him by wealth, abundance, and cheerfulness. But those are just phony measures by which the world seeks to enslave us.

If wealth is gained at the expense of others, what good is it? If I can eat because another starves, what nourishment do I receive? If I must stifle the sadness and doubt that life inevitably stirs in order not to bother anyone, what does my smile mean?

No, life proceeds by different measures. When we meet God "face to face," as a reader puts it, I believe the first word from God will be, "Welcome." No amount of spending or saving can change that welcome.

Out of God's special heart for the poor and suffering, God will talk with us about those times when we were poor and wounded. If any abrasions remain, they will be healed.

I believe God isn't the least interested in our wealth or success, except to wonder how much of life we sacrificed to attain it. Perhaps God will recite those times when we gave up family, health, and honor in order to get ahead, and we will ask God to remove our burden of regret.

I believe that alongside us in God's presence will stand the wretched of the earth, whose dingy, battered state we spent a lifetime trying to avoid. We will wonder why we didn't see them sooner. We will be humbled, they will be exalted, and then we will sit down together at God's table.

If we could imagine that banquet, I think we would relax our acquisitive instincts and allow nobility of character to flourish. We would see

Jesus standing on the plain, surrounded by the hungry and troubled. We would hear him inviting us to join him there. Not in that noblesse oblige which tends to guide Christian charity, but in recognition that here on the plain is truth—truth about God and about ourselves.

We might cling to our hillside, for it seems safer there. We might prefer to schedule our kindness around work. We might display our credentials and trophies, for they separate us from the herd. We might put gold on our altars, for God's favor might be for sale.

We might assemble the perfect package—wealth, accomplishment, happiness—but not likely, and certainly not forever.

Better to hear now our Lord's invitation to leave the hillside, accept our neediness, set aside our proofs of worthiness, and join him in that blessedness which we cannot buy or earn.

QUESTION 41: "What is God's purpose for me as I travel this journey, and how do I know the difference between God's will and the will of others, or even myself? Is everything I ever thought, did, or believed worthless? False?"

> *[A man] divided his property between [two sons]. A few days later the younger son gathered all he had and traveled to a distant country, and there he squandered his property in dissolute living.* (Luke 15:12–13)

After a pleasant round of golf, I joined a small crowd to watch the final minutes of the Duke-Maryland basketball game.

Duke blew a lead, Maryland forced overtime. It should have been gripping. But the referees had taken over the game, calling cheap fouls, ending almost every possession at the foul line. Enough of this, I said to myself.

When I stood to depart, a group said, almost in unison, "You're leaving?"

"This is too aggravating," I explained. But they were aghast. How could I turn away from something they found important?

I doubt that the ripple of my leaving had lasting impact. At any rational level, what does it matter whether I value what they value? But at the subrational level, where self and other collide, where emotion and need influence the ego, their instinctive reaction was to be disturbed, as if my leaving were judgment of their staying.

I have the same feeling when I enter a movie theater and find it empty. Have I missed something? It is difficult to think for yourself and to find yourself alone, moving in an opposite direction from others, at odds with trendsetters, having beliefs that the prevailing culture discourages.

It is tempting to label this "groupthink" and to disparage it. But it is normal to be sensitive to people around us, especially when their behaviors differ from our own. Hence the power of fashion and trends.

A reader asks about discerning purpose. How can she tell the difference between God's will and the will of others? An important question, and not easy to answer.

She needs to sort through groupthink, for one thing. The fact that "everyone else" values something—like seeing a movie—doesn't mean she should see it. Opinion leaders are simply shaping opinion, not necessarily speaking wisdom.

She needs to step beyond group response, that visceral tendency of groups to enforce their norms by any means. For group response leads quickly to group rage, when the threatened find common cause in punishing the perceived cause of danger.

Religion tends to encourage groupthink, group response, and group rage. For while we talk of having a "personal relationship" with God, our deeper need is to think, feel, behave, and believe alike. Any divergence casts doubt, and our faith doesn't have much room for doubt.

We gather with like-minded believers, we glare at the freethinker, we dispute divergent interpretations, we use verbal and physical violence against opposing opinion, and we claim our multitude as proof.

We need to read Jesus' parable of the prodigal son. The parable ends with the father's astonishing forgiveness and the older brother's jealousy. But how did the younger son get into such a mess? By going along with the crowd. He went to "a distant country," where people had different values. He was weak. He forgot his father's ways. He adapted. As long as his funds lasted, he could afford dissolution. But when a famine came, he had nothing substantial.

It was then that he "came to himself," Jesus said, and decided to go home, a humbling journey that all of us have made at one time. Not that the future is found by backpedaling, but that some places are healthier than others, some people nobler, some causes more worthy, some behaviors more godly.

As long as we are simply going along with the crowd—even with a crowd that claims holiness and right opinion—we remain lost. We must think for ourselves.

Chapter 5

Faith

QUESTION 42: "Jesus, why were you so focused on the kingdom of God?"

[Jesus said,] "When you see these things taking place, you know that the kingdom of God is near." (Luke 21:31)

My twenty-three-year-old son and I take San Angelo bars in hand, bend our shoulders to the task, and set about moving a dozen large stones into position.

We take turns prying and lifting, prying and lifting, until the stone makes a half turn, and we start again, shoulder touching shoulder, in a brute-force ballet that countless sons and fathers have done before us.

Wanting to do his part, wishing he were older and stronger, my youngest son moves smaller rocks. My wife applauds our efforts. Her father watches quietly. He recently left a Colonial-era farm where stone walls like this were 225 years old, and no one remembers who built them in that era when a cleared field meant crops and life, not scenery.

Next spring, we will plant a maple tree on one side of the stone wall and crepe myrtles and blueberry bushes on the other. Some day wall, trees, and shrubs will lie down in harmony. Today stones look raw and impermanent.

Later, three generations gather in front of the fireplace to read, to write, and to listen to *A Prairie Home Companion* on the radio. We are at peace.

And yet, as I listen to a duet broadcast from San Luis Obispo, California, I sense an ephemeral quality. The beauty of this duet took years of preparation, hours of rehearsal, and it is over in three minutes.

The novels we are devouring took months to write, and we race through them, as if they were an empty highway with no speed limit.

My wife, who is knitting an afghan for her father, tries to engage me in conversation about Christmas gifts for family. But I am too distracted by radio, novel, and sleepiness to respond. The moment will pass, and later I will regret not having responded.

Even love seems ephemeral, even beauty, even the joy of family, even warmth beside the fire. Like the Hebrews in the wilderness, I will arise tomorrow hungry again, wondering what happened to yesterday's abundance. I won't need to be morose or fatalistic to find myself asking, "What is the point?" For if you notice any beauty, you also notice beauty passing away, moments ending, time racing by, faces aging, chairs emptying.

Why did Jesus focus on the kingdom of God? Maybe, as Christian triumphalism has tended to assert, he was declaring victory, naming the prize to be won, assuring his followers that the garland would be theirs. They could stop time, seize eternity, so build those walls, high and to the sky. No tents in the desert for God's victorious tribe.

I think Jesus had a less prideful, less desperate message. I think he was saying time belongs to God, and when things come to pass— good things, bad things, victory things, defeat things, life things, death things—we can live and let go and trust in God to give our lives purpose.

We can listen to a radio broadcast, enjoy a lovely song, let it float beyond hearing, and not need it to be permanent. We can miss a caring moment and trust that love will try again. We can plant a tree for someone else to enjoy. We can see the moment and also its glow fading, and not feel betrayed by time.

It isn't up to us to make life worth living. We can only do our best to live the day. It is God who takes our days, adds them to other days, and writes a book for tomorrow to read. That is the "kingdom" which comes near. And as he faced the end of his own brief flowering and sent his friends forth for theirs, Jesus gave all of their days back to God.

QUESTION 43: "How should I respond to fundamentalist Christians who do not leave any room for doubt?"

[John said to the crowds,] "Do not begin to say to yourselves, 'We have Abraham as our ancestor'; for I tell you, God is able from these stones to raise up children to Abraham." (Luke 3:8)

We fill the conference room to hear about our new 401(k) retirement plan.

I ask a question. Inflation is low. But massive budget deficits and trade deficits, giveaways to the superrich, an unfunded war, and an administration that seems incompetent in basic governance could produce galloping inflation. Would bond funds still be an attractive investment? His answer: No, bonds are poised to tank.

My question is blatantly political, of course, reflecting my dim view of current leadership. Some at the table dispute my viewpoint, as well they might. Political opinions run the gamut. But they can't deny the sincerity of my question or my right to ask it.

In a healthy democratic system, people assess realities, run perceptions through a sieve of values, disagree openly, consider new information, vote, trust outcomes, and hang together.

In an unhealthy system, people succumb to comforting illusions, filter perceptions through group prejudices, declaim and demand without room for debate, focus relentless energy on single issues, and reject divergent outcomes.

Relentless and narrow focus wins battles, but at the expense of turning democracy and faith community into winner-take-all, zero-sum contests, a world of black and white, good guys and bad guys, worthy and unworthy.

In that world, there is no compromise, just a pious determination to press on until I get my way, because any other way is evil. There is no agreeing to disagree, but a fundamental disrespect for the other. There is no search for common ground, but a dogged probing for weakness. There is no perspective, but an unyielding fixation on the single issue. There is no moving on, but a steady amassing of forces.

We live in such a world now. Arguments never end, because they aren't allowed to end. Clever ideologues have hijacked politics and religion, taking political, ethical, and spiritual viewpoints, personal and cultural angst, and everyday questions, and creating a toxic brew that poisons the air. Foreign policy becomes spiritual war. Church disputes become absolutist battles—not the normal clash of diverse people struggling to comprehend God, but desperate warfare where defeat is perceived as dooming the Christian enterprise.

Ideologues keep repeating, "I am right, I am right, I am right." They quote Scriptures, political authorities, and statistics with a relentless determination to win, not to attain wisdom. Disprove one fact, and they find another. Articulate a convincing argument, and they condemn you as evil. Venture into ambiguity, and they pounce on your weakness.

Open your arms to embrace an opponent, and they respond with triumphant intolerance. Take a vote, and they reject as demonic any outcome but theirs.

This isn't a matter of conservative versus liberal, Republican versus Democrat, orthodox versus reform. Relentless ideologues arise in every camp. It is breakdown in civility, inability to resolve disputes, and ultimately collapse in basic democracy. For democracy depends on respect, common sense, and tolerance. But when respect is fundamentally denied, when common sense is viewed as moral weakness and tolerance as conspiring with evil, then the system collapses.

What do you say to the fundamentalist who leaves no room for doubt? The same thing you say to the fundamentalist's unyielding opponent. The same thing you say to the Christian zealot and the Islamic zealot. The same thing you say to the Republican ideologue and the Democratic ideologue.

Combining the thoughts of John and Paul, you say: Don't keep insisting you are right and all others wrong. God can raise up right opinion from these stones. If you don't love your neighbor, welcome the outcast, grant respect to your enemy, and yearn for God's peace, then your relentless pursuit of victory can only destroy.

QUESTION 44: "We are not to be foolish and follow every charismatic leader that has a compelling story to tell. How do we know the difference? How do we know the truth?"

The people were filled with expectation, and all were questioning in their hearts concerning John, whether he might be the Messiah. (Luke 3:15)

Let's cut to the chase. Here's mine.

I leave this morning to visit my ailing mother. The family is gathering. It is an important time.

At work we are engaged in important conversations about roles and values, and we are pursuing exciting opportunities. I find it energizing.

My sons are going through important transitions: schooling, career, relationships. When we gather for Christmas, the air will be filled with dynamic tensions.

I don't have time for nonsense. I don't mean to sound self-important. I just have no ear left for schlock seasonal music, for I want my ears to hear my mother's failing voice, my family's needs, my own heart, the cries of a troubled world.

I have no patience left for religious controversies that hijack my church at precisely the time when I need it most, for I need comfort, not doctrine; I need pastors who visit their flocks, not warriors in denominational battle; I need people who believe, not people who parade.

I have no appetite left for the ways I typically protect myself, for I don't want to be safe behind a wall. I want to see God's manna waiting on the desert floor. If that means I need to feel anguish, vexation, exhilaration, then so be it. I need to get out of my own way.

That's my chase. Your chase will be different. But I suspect we share a common desire to get real, to get beyond the reach of that which would divert our attention, exploit our neediness, seize our loyalties, corrode our goodwill, and turn our naïveté and gentleness against us.

We all live in what John calls "expectation." We scan the horizon for signs of hope and meaning. Out there, watching us scan, are predators, would-be messiahs, false prophets, people with a keen eye for our hungers and clever plans for exploiting us. They claim to offer easy answers. They claim to offer truth. They lie.

How, as the reader asks, can we tell the difference and avoid getting sucked into someone else's self-serving lie?

First, know our neediness. Our neediness makes us vulnerable and exploitable, but it also makes us human and is the starting point on our journey to hope. Our neediness has content—not just vague anxiety that a candy bar will soothe, but details, experiences, people, disappointments, wounds. We need to know ourselves better than we do.

Second, honor our worthiness. Predators want us to feel small and scared, charismatic leaders want us to buy their phony self-worth package, abusers want us to feel worthless. Those are lies.

Third, accept our unique and rough edges. Doctrinal warriors want us to believe diversity is dangerous. In fact, God loves what God made.

Fourth, believe in God's durability. God isn't offended by our neediness, or by our questioning, or by our following different paths. God is larger than that, stronger than that.

Fifth, abandon the illusion of a single "truth." God spoke in a dozen different voices just to the Hebrews. Imagine how many voices and stories God has used to reach the vastness of humanity. Moreover, God keeps on changing, responding, loving. Stories get updated. Words acquire new meanings. That isn't threatening to God. Why should it be threatening to us?

Finally, follow God, not the person claiming to speak for God. We have to work at it, but God can be known and heard, even by fools like us. Yes, we will know and hear different things, and our ways of following will be myriad. But that is truer to God's nature than one-size-fits-all.

QUESTION 45: "Can you go to heaven if you don't claim Jesus as your savior?"

[John said,] "He will baptize you with the Holy Spirit and fire. His winnowing fork is in his hand, to clear his threshing floor and to gather the wheat into his granary; but the chaff he will burn with unquenchable fire." (Luke 3:16–17)

My mother sits up as long as she can. Talking is tiring, so mainly she listens as we talk and play Scrabble.

She declines a drive downtown to look at "the world's tallest Christmas tree." She lies down, a serene smile on her face. She seems at peace.

I find it difficult to imagine that, as dying time nears, God is preparing an immigration desk where she will need to prove her worthiness, where some documentation like a baptismal certificate or signed creed will be required before she can proceed to live with God. I can imagine people setting up such a process, because the threat of hell and promise of heaven are potent weapons in subjugating humankind. But not God.

I know that flies in the face of every religion's assertions that its way is the only way. But think about it. Why would God create a lovely woman, carry her steadfastly through life, and then abandon her at the last minute? Why would God allow litmus tests developed by expansionist religions to determine whom God can and cannot love? Why would the God who brought exiles out of bondage suddenly, as home came into view, turn into a petty bureaucrat with a form to fill out? Or a snob with breeding papers to authenticate?

It makes no sense. It makes God too small, too mean. Maybe we need to allow another possibility—that we don't understand. We think we understand, we want to have it nailed down, our theologians and prelates insist they know, but maybe we are so concerned with making God our partisan that we miss God's point.

Take, for example, the "unquenchable fire" promised by John and much beloved of hellfire-warning preachers. That image—messiah separating humankind into two piles and burning one of them—has delighted every major religion and justified countless religious wars.

But maybe John meant this:

Messiah came to lead exiles home from bondage. To leave the safety of captivity, they must leave many things behind, even those treasures that they thought necessary.

Hence the two piles: what we truly need, and what we must leave behind. Messiah helps us to see the difference. For we get wants and needs confused, we allow things to define us, we want too much comfort and certainty, and so the pile to carry onward tends to be too large.

Wasn't that the teaching of Jesus? Die to self, give wealth away, give up hating your enemy, let go of fear, let go of old ways. Instead, cast off your old garments, and come to God as an innocent child. Interestingly, Islam has exactly the same teachings.

That is the "unquenchable fire": God's unyielding determination to love humanity and to lead humanity out of bondage. An iron will for justice and acceptance. A zeal for seeing with merciful eyes, not with the prideful filters of humanity. A heart for love, not for hate. A mind that saw beyond the shallow moment—that bade Mary of Bethany come close for learning, even if that violated norms; that embraced outcasts and sinners, even if that offended the scorecard-wielding righteous.

Maybe the chaff is what we must leave behind. Maybe it takes a lifetime to figure out what is chaff. Maybe my mother's smile isn't defeat, but victory, a shedding of load.

Maybe it hurts like hell for us to spend lifetimes amassing treasures and then to discover that they don't matter. But to judge by my mother's serenity, it can be a relief to have the threshing floor cleared.

QUESTION 46: "Jesus, Son of David, turn my daughter's search for acceptance from drugs and promiscuity to your loving embrace."

What has come into being in him was life, and the life was the light of all people. The light shines in the darkness, and the darkness did not overcome it. (John 1:3–5)

Tonight, some will gather with family in the glow of candles, and some will sit alone in the flicker of a television set.

Tonight, some will look around tables and be glad for the blessings of life, and some will look at family members who hurt them.

Tonight, some will have a glass of wine and stop, and some will continue drinking until this night ends the way most nights end.

Tonight, some will worship God in cheerful places, and some will taste the acid of their alienation from church or from God.

Tonight, some children will go to bed excited, and some will listen to gunfire and shouting outside their bedrooms.

Tonight, some will turn off the lights of home in anticipation of a merry Christmas, and some will stand guard far from home in anticipation of warfare's unceasing mayhem.

Tonight, some will stay close to heart and hearth, and some will prowl the clubs and streets, looking for thrills or escape or, as in the case of this reader's daughter, "acceptance."

It is necessary that we know all that is going on. God surely does. For it was this chasm in the human experience that Jesus came to redeem, this exile called loneliness, or addiction, or alienation, or warfare.

Jesus was light shining in the darkness, as John put it. A messiah sent to lead God's people out of bondage and home across a fearsome desert, as Luke put it. A shepherd for the lost sheep, as Matthew put it.

The birth of Jesus makes no sense apart from the darkness. There can be no understanding this moment, and no celebrating it, unless we see the lost and lonely, the child crouching in terror, the soldier far from home, the trapped digging their pit deeper. Our seasonal bustle is madness unless we acknowledge the darkness we are trying to escape.

If we could listen in on Christmas prayers and hear what God hears, I think we would hear a mother's cry—save my daughter from herself! We would hear the elderly begging companionship. We would hear children like myself wishing we could be near our dying parents. We would hear the clanking chains of injustice that drag down more lives than we realize. We would hear the desperation, the confusion, the fear that lie within modern religion's trivial conflicts.

We would hear the pastor sitting alone in the darkness with a thousand wounds, a thousand painful memories, a thousand cries of need, a thousand burdens unknown by anyone else and unshared, and we would see the pastor searching for the right words, hoping that this year the convivial will listen, the smug will stop judging, and the lost sheep will come home.

We would hear the organist practicing alone in a darkened chancel, playing fingers gently over the keyboard, searching for the right touch that will enable the faithful not to bellow "O come all ye faithful," but to caress it, to feel it, to mean it.

None of this makes any sense unless we can acknowledge the darkness and ourselves as "people who walk in darkness." Jesus was light in the darkness, not a cheerleader for the pious. Jesus was light in the darkness, not a proud institution's poster child. Jesus was light in the darkness, not a fastidious dispenser of tidy rules and well-deserved rewards.

To a mother who sees her daughter walking in darkness, and to every one of us in that darkness which we hesitate to admit, Jesus was—and is today—that light which the darkness cannot vanquish.

QUESTION 47: "Why are we so blind? Why is it so hard for us to see?"

[John] came as a witness to testify to the light, so that all might believe through him. He himself was not the light, but he came to testify to the light. (John 1:7–8)

Today will be confusing for many people.

Some children will race through opening presents and ask, "Is that all there is?" They will be perplexed as to why the cornucopia runs dry. Is there some boundary to parental power, Santa's generosity, or their worthiness that they hadn't known about?

Other children will sense through endless advertisements that theirs is a meager holiday. They, too, will ask, Why?

With expectation at unusual heights, lovers won't quite connect with the gifts they give and the plans they make. They will have wanted more or different, some assurances that they weren't aware of needing.

Others won't be connecting at all. Christmas is that time when frayed relationships cannot be hidden, when being alone hurts, when the ghosts of yesterday seem cruel companions.

It is a time for families to gather and for neighbors to need each other, and for everyone to be patient and kind, willing to give more than they receive. Some will muster that grace, but many will discover that Christmas doesn't rescue a family, as much as expose its need for rescue.

I remember driving home from the choral Eucharist several years ago. I had watched the church go from empty to full to empty again, from silent to boisterous to silent again. The music minister had found just the right touch for "Adeste Fideles," the choir had sung beyond themselves. Hundreds had been fed before a blazing bank of flowers. I closed the doors, walked to an empty parking lot, and felt that letdown which comes after large events.

It was 1 A.M. My family was asleep. I felt alone. Then I turned onto my street and came upon a highway of candles. Neighbors had lighted these luminaries hours before, but they still burned bright. Their glow led me home.

A reader asks why it is so hard for us to see. There is no one answer, of course. Some are lost in sin, some are victims of darkness being visited upon them, some are trapped inside themselves, some are confused.

We can know this: If seeing were easy, God wouldn't have bothered to give his Son, and Jesus wouldn't have needed to die, and the Spirit wouldn't have been sent to hover over life from now to eternity. If seeing were easy, choirs wouldn't need to sing, organists wouldn't rehearse when no one notices, giving souls wouldn't prepare altars, donate flowers, show pilgrims to their seats, touch the shoulder of one crying softly, or kneel before God's table and beg food that they cannot give themselves.

If seeing were easy, I would drive alone and not think a thing about it. If seeing were easy, candles wouldn't take my breath away, and the sight of loved ones sleeping trustingly wouldn't stagger my heart.

If the false luminaries of this world could cast real light, then we could bask in whatever glow is available and not be confused by what isn't yet being seen. We wouldn't notice our child's frown or our lover's grimace. We wouldn't notice the empty chair or the widow's sigh. We wouldn't notice anything that disturbed the smooth perfection of a man-made Christmas.

God's witnesses, however, are never content to let us be. Like John, they urge us to see, but also remind us that the light we give ourselves isn't real light, and what we think we see—and take pride in seeing—might not be anything more than shadows on a wall.

To see anything, we need to see it all. And that gets confusing.

Here, then, is a Christmas toast to seeing it all!

QUESTION 48: "If I encountered Jesus, I honestly do not know what I would ask."

The law indeed was given through Moses; grace and truth came through Jesus Christ. (John 1:17)

I thought I had this day figured out.

Plant forsythia, and get ready for spring. Play golf, and recover from yesterday's abysmal outing. Enjoy an evening with the family and *A Prairie Home Companion*.

Planting proves exhausting. I need my wife's help to plant six evergreen shrubs and my neighbor's help to relocate a huge forsythia bush. Instead of a warm glow, I end up covered with dirt and depleted of all strength.

On the golf course, I am arm-weary. I lower my expectations. Sure enough, I have my best round all year.

We discover that *Prairie Home* is still on the road in New York City, where host Garrison Keillor lets himself get intimidated by Big Apple "sophistication" and offers shows that are too clever, too snazzy, too urban. I groan.

The day ends on a surreal note with a viewing of *The Graduate*, the 1967 film that, for me at least, affirmed California as weird, young adult-hood as confusing, Katharine Ross as unappealing, Simon & Garfunkel as saccharine, sports cars as embodying freedom, and cinema as a brilliant art form.

What happened to the orderly day I had mapped out? Here, in a homely nutshell, is the clash between law and grace.

Law seeks to bring order to the chaos. Its basic promise is that the wild can be tamed; the human will can be channeled; passions can be controlled; yesterday can be explained, today planned, and tomorrow trusted.

In Torah, Moses made it possible for newly liberated slaves to cross a desert, to claim a promised land, and to set about forming a nation. Law gave them stories to be used again and again, structure for a theocratic society, and clear guidelines for what is pleasing to God. A people of the law knew what questions to ask, as well as how truthful answers would sound.

When Israel's history proved at variance with the law, authors added new codes, as if the Yahweh of the confident Davidic era and the granularity—the fine detail—of the postexile rulebook were all parts of one sweeping whole.

Jesus represented an entirely new voice. Not law, but grace. Not order, but surprise. Not precise definition, but ambiguous parable. Not a power hierarchy grounded in interpreting and enforcing laws, but a free-floating circle with no specific shape. Not a codification of truth, but the gift of sight. Not control leading to victory, but servanthood leading to sacrifice.

The author of John saw this and produced a book of stories, or "signs," in which grace and truth would be revealed not so much in the healing of the man born blind, but in his surprising encounter afterward with the religious establishment. Instead of the law's invitation to study and to obey, Jesus invited Nathanael to "come and see."

Christians have never been entirely comfortable with grace. We keep turning to legalism and doctrine, as if pure sight cannot be trusted. Our quest, of course, is control. We want to plan our days, as it were. We want our assemblies to be orderly, our boundaries clearly marked, our songs tasteful, our pathways to inclusion and salvation well defined. Much of the turmoil in modern Christianity starts here, in the quest for control through legalism.

Life, however, is far too wild for that. This plan-confounding day is just further proof that I have no more control over events than Benjamin

Braddock had over Mrs. Robinson. The reader who doesn't know what question she would ask of Jesus is simply being true to life's weird and uncharted nature.

Our obsession with hemming each other in does little more than reveal our shallowness. Jesus stepped away from the law, thereby offending the legalists and bringing about his downfall.

QUESTION 49: "What is the purpose of life? The meaning of it all?"

When Herod died, an angel of the Lord suddenly appeared in a dream to Joseph in Egypt and said, "Get up, take the child and his mother, and go to the land of Israel, for those who were seeking the child's life are dead." (Matthew 2:19–20)

Diversionary maneuvers will abound in the coming year. That's my prediction.

In a presidential election year, politicians will divert public attention away from their failings and self-serving. Through ads, clever titles for legislation, well-managed photo ops and speeches, and gratuitous attacks on opponents, they will seek to be what they are not.

The weak will want to appear strong. The elitist will want to show a common touch. Those who are crippling social services will talk of "tax reform." Show-investigations will promise action that no one intends to take. Contracts will go to cronies, while officials dismiss critics as unpatriotic.

Leaders of the economy will keep the shells moving. Undercount the jobless, don't notice when corporations ship jobs overseas, ignore executive compensation, minimize innovation and capital spending, fight regulations, do anything to boost stock prices.

Educators will test, rather than teach, and call it "leaving no child behind." Moviemakers will crowd their few quality pictures into Oscar-minded releases, while continuing their profitable degrading of an art form. Television will continue its relentless coarsening of the culture. Abusers will blame their victims, adulterers will blame their spouses, and lazy students will blame their teachers.

And religion, which should be in the business of seeing all this and offering higher purposes, will talk of little but sex. Congregations and denominations will continue to fracture over homosexuality. Even parish elections will turn on sexuality-based litmus tests.

Woe betide anyone who rains on these diversionary parades. A politician who spoke honestly to what is on people's minds would be mocked offstage. Bonuses and advancement are denied to people who question leaders. Preachers who delve into political, economic, and cultural issues are admonished to mind their own business.

What do I wish would happen? I wish people could hear the questions posed by this reader: What is purpose? What is meaning? Those are the questions that occupy our hearts in the night watch and greet us upon arising.

Who awakens wondering what the bishop thinks about sex? Or what outfit the president wore to a photo op? Or who scored bonuses when the Dow stayed above 10,000? Or how many cents did Wal-Mart shave off T-shirts today?

We have this one life to live, and much of it is difficult. We deal with wrenching issues like loneliness, illness, distance, empty relationships, economic deprivation, and fear. Many of us awaken to injustice. Even when the tide is going our way, we know it will turn, and we wonder what is the purpose of such ebbing and flowing.

I don't expect politicians, business leaders, cultural icons, or educators to address these issues. But I do expect faith communities to make the effort. Otherwise, why are we in business? If we cannot help our communities wrestle with issues of purpose and meaning, we should give back our tax exemptions and trust funds, yield our prime real estate to commerce, and stop pretending to care about salvation.

For salvation isn't about denominational attitudes on sex. Talk about parades that need raining on. Salvation is about despots like King Herod, systems that allow a few to prosper while many suffer, and predators who steal time and joy. That means politics, economics, and culture—the very forces that Jesus came to redirect, the very forces that crushed him.

Purpose and meaning arise out of the complex interplay of work, relationships, duty, justice, freedom, faith, and hope. I cannot give a pat answer to today's reader. I can wish that her pastor and Christianity in general wouldn't waste another year in diversions, but would venture onto dangerous ground, as Joseph, Mary, and Jesus ventured to Israel.

QUESTION 50: "How do I discern what is my wisdom and yours?"

The steward tasted the water that had become wine, and did not know where it came from (though the servants who had drawn the water knew). (John 2:9)

Our new neighbors pick up our mail and newspapers while we are away at a funeral and send us a sympathy card on our return.

No big deal, you say—that is what neighbors do. Well, is it? Over the years, I have had neighbors who never spoke, who called the police when my son had a reasonably normal teenage party, who cut down my cherry trees at night and then drunkenly challenged me to a fight, who crossed to the other side of the street when they saw me coming, who took but never gave.

I have also had neighbors who were kind, who shared hurricane recovery, who looked after our children, who watched our house during vacations, who were happy to exchange dinner invitations, who brought food when tragedy struck, who stood at the fence and chatted.

Both kinds are real. How do I know which are a reflection of my worth? Which are from God?

You can't just measure the evidence. Only three of my mother's immediate neighbors attended her funeral, out of perhaps sixty people who live nearby. What does a 95 percent no-show rate mean? Nothing, probably, but how do I know?

You can't just notice the pleasant. Sometimes a frosty neighbor is an accurate reflection of your own neighborliness. The hard-to-hear word sometimes is the true word.

You can't just intellectualize the situation and explain unfriendliness by pointing, say, to studies of urban life, or the isolating impact of television, or the neighbor's moral or emotional deficits. Those are factors. But some rise above them. Why don't others?

You can't just turn to a trustworthy source of authority such as Scripture and by prowling the word find the passages that turn the lens to clarity. Too much self-selection in what you choose to notice.

Nor, it seems, can you guarantee better results by moving to a new place, trying on new behaviors, or being patient with what is.

My best answer is this: first, listen to life. Listen to all of life. Listen to the hard-to-hear word and to the pleasant. Listen to the friendly neighbor and the unfriendly. Listen to the dull and the sharp, to the friend and the enemy. Take it all in. At the risk of overload and confusion, be an avid witness of the disorderly swirl.

Second, be wary of filters. Inherited wisdom might be little more than mossy prejudice. What feels good might be delusional. Even instinct and intuition can lead astray.

Third, be prepared for trial and error. Discernment takes effort and engagement. To see anything is to see everything; to consider one new idea is to countenance many new ideas. And we are likely to get it wrong. We will hear what sounds wrong, raise our defenses against it, and only discover later that it was right. Or vice versa.

The wine steward at the wedding in Cana didn't know all that was happening. The servants knew one additional detail but not the whole story. The bridegroom was clueless. Even the author of John's Gospel saw only in part. The meaning of this sign would take centuries to emerge—and is still emerging in our day.

Perhaps the bottom-line answer to the reader's question to God— "How do I discern what is my wisdom and yours?"—is this: with humility. You discern with humility. Our enemy in discernment isn't error, but pride, arrogance, and defensiveness.

QUESTION 51: "Do we who call ourselves Christians get to 'pick and chose' what we want to do/believe?"

[Jesus] rolled up the scroll, gave it back to the attendant, and sat down. The eyes of all in the synagogue were fixed on him. (Luke 4:20)

I own a dozen Bibles.

One, a King James Version, was a gift for college. I rarely consulted it, but I placed its black ribbon at Isaiah 11, where a vision of paradise regained fed my 1960s idealism.

I bought several in seminary, all heavy Bibles with study notes. It was probably a New English Bible that I was reading on that magical day when, while grappling with Mark 10:46–52, a lens turned and the Scripture came alive to me.

The one I use daily is a leather-bound New Revised Standard Version that shows the stains and rips of being flipped through while preaching. I yield nothing to the fundamentalist preachers who wave their Bibles, like Senator McCarthy waving his files, and claim to know it all.

In their "roadside questions," many readers asked about the Bible and its authority. Some are confused by allegations that there is a single "biblical faith" and that this belief system clearly condemns this and requires that. Some find themselves demeaned by that "biblical faith." Some wonder why the Bible is used to justify division and hatred.

One reader is close to quitting her Bible study group because she cannot reconcile the commandment not to kill with passages where God commands killing. I responded:

"The Bible contains many contradictions. That is one problem with the fundamentalists' determination to harvest quotes and to treat them all the same.

"The Bible is more like a living person, or the story of a large family. Some parts don't gibe with others, and some stories get told from multiple perspectives and sound different each time. But if you read the Bible as showing the trajectory, complexity, tragedy, and joy of humanity's journey with God, the books start to come alive."

Rather than let fundamentalists continue to hijack Scripture as their particular property and as meaning only the one thing they say it means, all Christians need to do their own reading of Scripture.

It isn't easy, but it isn't impossible. If a believer wants a solid foundation, I think Scripture has to be taken seriously. For the answer to the reader's question, you see, is, Yes, we do "pick and choose" what to believe. It isn't that we "get to," but that we have no other choice.

People make many assertions about God, Jesus, Spirit, church, human life, sin, and hope—assertions that cannot possibly all be true. Virtually every one of those assertions can be buttressed by reference to Scripture, even the most outlandish. If you are willing to think creatively about Scripture—to read between the lines, to notice what isn't said, to plumb the emotions and motivations on display for additional meaning —you can assert anything and defend it.

That is maddening to those who want an easy faith, to those who build brilliant careers on offering an easy faith, and to those who have arrived at a particular political or moral conclusion and want to impose that conclusion on everyone else. But so it goes.

The Bible was never intended to be a rule book, instruction manual, or objective history. It is many stories about God told by certain branches of humanity over a period of some 1,100 years. Other stories can be told about that God and that period, other branches of humanity tell their own stories, and a lot has been written, sung, prayed, and lived in the past 2,000 years.

Sorting through these stories and discerning the God who lies behind them can be an exciting journey. But you have to allow the pages to get dirty, and you have to allow room for other people to find different meanings.

QUESTION 52: "Is IT really true?"

[Jesus] began to say to them, "Today this scripture has been fulfilled in your hearing." (Luke 4:21)

A "winter storm watch" courses through our Southern city.

Northerners would be amused by what we consider worth watching. (One inch of snow?) Nevertheless, the watch is issued, and people immediately respond to it.

Radio and television meteorologists move to center stage. Grocery aisles fill. Sunday plans change. People stockpile water, in case electricity goes out.

Is it true? Well, prediction of the storm certainly is true, and people's immediate response to warnings is true. Whether the storm itself proves true remains to be seen. As Doris Day sang in 1956 for an Alfred Hitchcock film, "What will be, will be."

Given the opportunity to pose a "roadside question" to Jesus, a reader asks, "Is it really true?" She doesn't define "it," but that just makes the question reverberate all the more. Take Luke's recounting of the day Jesus brought truth to his hometown.

Invited to teach at his family synagogue, Jesus stood up to read Isaiah's assurance that God was redeeming the poor, the captives, and the blind, an ancient truth much loved for its comfort. But when he sat down to teach, reality shifted. "Today," he said, "this scripture has been fulfilled in your hearing."

Like a winter storm, that word grew in severity. His townsfolk first thought him gracious, but then they recognized that not only was he casting them as poor, captive, and blind, but he was declaring the moment as now, not safely in the past, and himself as the agent. That immediacy stunned them. Truth went from safe to dangerous, from distant to present, from vague to personal.

The people of Nazareth immediately took arms against his troubling truth. They couldn't stop it, but they did change it. For now Jesus recognized a truth he hadn't seen before: "No prophet is accepted in the prophet's hometown." That truth, in turn, would come to dominate his ministry, as he adjusted to rejection, became a wanderer, avoided Jerusalem until the time was right, and recruited disciples to carry on what he saw would be a short-lived ministry.

The answer is, Yes, it is true. But then you have to grapple with the fullness of "it." Yes, Jesus lived. Yes, we know something of his words and actions, and we know they got him killed. Yes, he rose from the dead. Yes, brave men and women carried on his ministry. Yes, they faced the same rejection that Jesus faced, and persecution changed their truth, as it had for Jesus.

Then truth gets muddy. Like a meteorologist seizing the microphone, early Christians made too much of the institution they were creating. They recited the good news spoken in Nazareth but lost touch with its truth. In their quest for power, they began to distance themselves from the poor, captive, and blind. They began to proclaim themselves.

Not content with the ambiguity of parables or the gradually unfolding nature of Jesus' ministry, they demanded concrete truth: doctrines, walls of separation, hierarchies of power, and rules. They asserted truths that were pleasing in their specificity and certainty but largely foreign to what Jesus actually said and did. We are still arguing over those derivative assertions.

I think Jesus would say to this reader, "Yes, what I said and did was true. But there was more, and that more still needs to be discerned."

Consider 1956. Would Doris Day have demanded a singing role if she had known her song would win an Oscar but spoil her dramatic film debut, forever miring her in sweetness? If Hitchcock had foreseen Elvis Presley's five number one hits in 1956, would he have done a different remake of *The Man Who Knew Too Much*?

Truth, you see, lies not only in the known, but in the mystery after "if."

QUESTION 53: "I would ask for forgiveness and mercy."

[Jesus] said to them, "Doubtless you will quote to me this proverb, 'Doctor, cure yourself!' And you will say, 'Do here also in your hometown the things that we have heard you did at Capernaum.'" (Luke 4:23)

Today's e-mail dialogue has a dreary predictability.

A reader of my newspaper column takes issue with last week's words. So far so good. Any newspaper column ought to provoke discussion.

But rather than state his opposing view, he challenges my faith and my right to have an opinion. I should let it drop, but I keep hoping for an ounce of reason. I reply that if he truly wants to know what I believe, I can send him these daily meditations.

He fires back: "That is what I thought. You do not want to know the truth. Whether you know it or not, there will be a judgment day. It WILL send sinners to hell! See you on judgment day!!!"

There you have it. Another glimpse of the great divide. Not just division of opinion, but condemnation of an opposing viewpoint, condemnation of a person, and a bedrock belief that all who disagree with him are bound for hell.

This is the fire that politicians play with as they insert religious issues like "marriage" into the presidential campaign. This is what happens when religion stops leading and simply follows potential contributors into loathing and bigotry. That is what ensues when church combatants behave like adolescents—shouting down "mean" parents, overstating wildly to gain negotiating room, deflecting attention from their angst—and get away with it.

Deep veins of hatred, violence, and bigotry probably lie within every one of us. Liberal and conservative, gay-affirming and gay-bashing, modernists and traditionalists, cheerful and embittered, young and old, wise and foolish—we all have our buttons. Push them, and we explode. This reader's venom is just a taste of the toxic stew that we could all spew out. His button is nearer the surface and more clearly labeled, that's all.

It's easy to counsel restraint and perspective. But self-restraint, self-respect, and self-control don't come easily, especially when putative leaders encourage extremes and the middle ground is labeled weak.

One great tragedy of history—which we seem doomed to repeat endlessly—is that Jesus saw this coming, he tried to show a different way, and yet in his name have come the worst excesses of zealotry, scapegoating, demonizing, demagoguery, and violence.

What did Jesus see? He saw his townsfolk rising up against him. It isn't entirely clear why. Something in his message—its immediacy perhaps, its naming them as needing salvation—something enraged them. He started to argue, but then "went on his way." Rather than smite them, he let them be.

This, not holy warfare, was his pattern. He taught and moved on. He risked enraging God's people, but restrained his own impulse to fire back. He had that impulse, as he showed in angry exchanges with his disciples, but he taught forgiveness and mercy. He taught forbearance. He taught love of enemy, not conquest. He lived what he taught.

Jesus knew that the love of God is strong. God doesn't require our weapons. God isn't made safe or believable by our violent words or deeds. Humanity's respect for God isn't promoted by holy warfare. God's existence doesn't depend on us, and God's will is far larger than our causes of the day. We might unleash our destructive passions in order to feel better, but we should be under no illusion that doing so serves God in any way.

My e-mail warrior views "judgment day" as the time of retribution. Maybe so. But I believe that when we meet the God of forgiveness and mercy, he will say to us all, "I tried to show you a better way. But it was too much for you. Well, you're home now, you're safe. Welcome."

QUESTION 54: "Does God care how I connect with him?"

Once while Jesus was standing beside the lake of Gennesaret, and the crowd was pressing in on him to hear the word of God, he saw two boats there at the shore of the lake; the fishermen had gone out of them and were washing their nets. (Luke 5:1–2)

What an interesting day!

We settle into our usual pew. Things are proceeding as usual, when the pastor's sermon ventures into deep water. His face and voice change, his words sound more serious. I suddenly feel more connected with other worshipers.

Later, we accompany our son to opening day at confirmation class. I don't have any particular expectations of confirmation. Rites of passage tend to happen again and again, not just the one official time. But I am delighted to see my boy connecting with ten other sixth-graders in a nurturing environment. I relax a little about the gauntlet of adolescence.

Next is a Super Bowl party. I rarely watch television sports, but I am pleased to spend an evening with friends. I nod off during the halftime show and miss the only moment anyone will remember—Janet Jackson's partial unveiling. The game is long and, despite our armchair critiquing, unsuccessful in outcome. But we connect family to family.

Some people take such connections for granted. Their every day is like this. But not mine. I am part of that legion that has moved too often and lost touch with friends in former places. To have a day like this leaves me smiling.

A reader asks if God cares how we "connect with him." My first response is, "Of course not. The point is to be close, not to do closeness correctly."

But I think we need to take it deeper, for many believe that God does care how we draw nigh. They point to the "narrow gate," to banquet doors being shut and correct attire being required, to the law and its stipulations. Religion tends to care deeply about procedures and protocols, as if celebrating the Eucharist incorrectly could drain it of meaning, as if religious argument must proceed in a certain way and achieve a certain outcome to avert "mortal sin," as if prayers said incorrectly wouldn't be heard.

In the Gospels, Jesus was on the move, going to people where they were, bringing his word and touch to the shores where they washed nets, to the houses and markets where they went about daily life. He sought people out.

When he found people, he touched their daily lives—like the time he helped Simon and friends fish more effectively—and he drew them into connection with each other. Rather than form a series of one-off links, like the family or company where one person tries to be the center of all relationships, Jesus gave people to one another.

When the religious insist on a single path—one way to read Scripture, one way to worship, one way to believe, one way to manage daily life—they don't get in God's way, for God will do what God will do, no matter what restrictions the righteous try to impose. But their prickliness and haughtiness do obstruct our connecting with one another. It isn't God who splinters churches, corrodes friendships, and creates dueling elites. It is our own narrow-mindedness and shallowness.

Such fishing will take us nowhere. It is time to cast our nets on the other side. Root for Patriots or Panthers, be shocked, amused, or bored by a rocker's unveiling, but look around at hearts and hands that want to connect as deeply as you do. That, I believe, is God's dream for us: connecting with decent people in a nurturing environment, without regard to litmus tests or narrow gates, and then inviting others, in their splendid diversity, to connect, as well.

QUESTION 55: "God, what will it take to get rid of the barriers between you and me?"

Now about eight days after these sayings Jesus took with him Peter and John and James, and went up on the mountain to pray. And while he was praying, the appearance of his face changed, and his clothes became dazzling white. (Luke 9:28–29)

My twenty-three-year-old son and I step outside after lunch, shiver in late-winter wind, and agree that it is too cold for golf.

But golf dates are hard to arrange. So, fifteen minutes later, we reassess and decide that it isn't too cold, after all.

When I emerge from the pro shop, however, a cold rain is starting, and predictions of sleet look accurate. Reality shifts again. No golf today.

Weather is relative, as are most things. This 42-degree day would seem balmy in New England, where the day's high was 13. If this were, say, Pinehurst No. 2 and we had called twelve months ago to reserve a tee time, we would play in anything short of snow.

Rather than insist that rain and 42 are "absolutely" wrong for golfing, we need to sort through not only the weather, but our mounting impatience with a long and stressful winter, indoor ways to spend time together, and the prediction of 60 degrees by Friday.

Other golfers, of course, are making different decisions. As we flee to comfort, I notice a foursome teeing off on 5.

A reader asks how to get closer to God, "to get rid of the barriers." Religion has no shortage of answers. Those answers disagree—hence denominations—but rarely fail to be absolute. Some say that God is absolute truth, that God is absolutely unchanging, that the Bible is God's definitive word, that anything found in Scripture is therefore absolute truth, and any other posture is sin.

Others dispute some or all of this logical string and arrive, predictably, at their own absolutes.

It is a tidy system all around. The obvious problem—that denominations stake out wildly contradictory positions—doesn't diminish believers' confidence in their own absolutes.

How else, they seem to say, could one believe? Is there any path to faith that doesn't make absolute claims about God? If your faith isn't grounded in absolutes, how do you know you aren't worshiping your own shadow or appetites?

Conservative and liberal Christians tend to shout at each across this divide. You're hopelessly relativistic, say fundamentalists. You're rigid and mindless, say liberals. I have taken my turn in this shouting match.

But as I spend time with the questions that truly reside in believers' hearts, I realize that such shouting succeeds in little more than hardening our hearts and convincing pilgrims that religion is a curse on the land. We have succeeded in causing a curious "reformation" that says, echoing Mercutio's dying gasp to Romeo, "A plague o' both your houses!"

The "barriers" between ourselves and God, you see, are always obstacles that we construct. God loves; it is we who hate. God is steadfast; it is we who resent and reject. God draws near; it is we who hide. God transfigured Jesus; it is we who refuse to change. God feeds freely; it is we who hoard. God welcomes a prodigal's return; it is we who stay stubbornly away.

The answer to this reader's question, therefore, is a call to self-examination. The question isn't whether 42 degrees is "absolutely" cold, but does it pose a barrier to me? What in this reader's life has become an obstacle? Scripture names numerous possibilities, from fear to pride, from illness to death, from lost hope to lost sight. But this reader must take her own journey inward.

Religion must argue less and examine more. We must help people to examine their lives, so that God can draw near. That won't build denomination or edifice, but it will serve God.

QUESTION 56: "Lord, what must I do today to be made whole, to see the light, so that I may be completely open to you, and say yes to whatever you ask of me?"

Now Peter and his companions were weighed down with sleep; but since they had stayed awake, they saw [Jesus'] glory and the two men who stood with him. (Luke 9:32)

Today blends into tomorrow as I pull into the garage, but the fact remains, this business trip began at 5 A.M. and ended nineteen hours, four airports, one decent omelet, and one tasteless pizza later.

Like Peter and his companions, I am "weighed down with sleep" as I reenter my home. I snoozed through entire states at 32,000 feet, managed to stay alert while waiting for my 10:15 P.M. flight in Atlanta, and now am thinking Nod.

But I do see one interesting piece of mail, from the publishing house that will put out a book of mine later this year. It turns out to be a sample of the book's cover art. For the first time I see its title in print, plus my name, all within a handsome graphic design. I am not too tired to smile.

A project that began as an idea and an invitation suddenly seems real, in the sense of concrete, physical, or to use a church term, "incarnational." It will happen, it will look like this, and it could have this range of impacts.

Those impacts, of course, are beyond my knowing. Like any author, I wonder if anyone will buy or read it. But even more, I will never know what happens to readers when they sit with my words and allow them inside. I believe that words transform lives. But writing and reading are mysterious processes.

So I see an idea taking shape, but most of what there is to see in the moment lies far ahead, around the bend, beyond my sight. I am seeing possibility more than anything else.

Simon Peter's struggle—shared by many believers—was to see his master transfigured and then immediately to grasp what he wasn't seeing. See the glory, and yet imagine that glory descending from the mountain and touching others. See Moses and Elijah standing with Jesus, and yet imagine a vast and scattered multitude one day doing the same.

Simon's struggle was to see possibility. Religion wants so badly to be concrete, literal, and as provable as any assertion of science. The belief seems to be that it is the actual, not the ideal, that has potency. We talk about faith as "belief in things unseen," but I don't think we are convinced.

I think we yearn for more tactile substance, more observable phenomena, more specifics.

But, to answer a reader's question, being "made whole," seeing the light and becoming open to God are a journey into the possible. It is today's glimpse taken around the bend. It is a glimpse of glory being allowed to scatter, like a cloud of perfume, touching and touching far beyond the wearer's passing.

To be made whole, we must see what there is to see, and then imagine that more lies ahead. It is to make restlessness, not certainty, one's attitude. It is to enjoy but even more to yearn.

Peter, of course, was unable to let any of this happen. His instinct was like that of every believer who built a building or wrote down a prayer or damned change for daring to occur. It was to freeze the moment, both to retain it and to stop its cloudlike scattering.

But there was a brief moment, before the control needs arose, when he simply saw the glory. Such moments aren't simple ecstasy, for they are incomplete in themselves, but they sure taste better than pizza in Oklahoma City.

QUESTION 57: "Why are we allowed so much FREE WILL?"

The devil said to [Jesus], "If you are the Son of God, command this stone to become a loaf of bread." Jesus answered him, "It is written, 'One does not live by bread alone.'" (Luke 4:3–4)

BOSTON—I sit in a conference room—beloved Boston beckoning me outside—and choose to focus on work.

All at the table are making choices: to speak or to stay silent, to listen or to control, to seek consensus or to command, to allow fresh vision or to recite stale ideas.

This is how business (or life) proceeds. It is how we define ourselves, remembering (or forgetting) who we are and discerning (or ignoring) where God is leading us. It is how we give (or deny) meaning to our time.

Someone could issue a decree. End the discussion, go straight to a solution, let us disband. But that would yield a meaningless outcome. Even more, it would cheapen our lives.

Or we could play adolescent games, snicker, pass notes, and engage in that triangulation, much beloved of the passive-aggressive, in which one says, "You know, Mary is very upset with you and doesn't want to talk with you.

"Don't tell her I told you."

Life is about choices. Faith is about choices. Some try to take away our choices, often doing so in the name of God. Some try to declare certain choices off-limits, usually choices that offend them or threaten their privilege. Some try to channel our choices into addictions, greed, hatred, conformity, or lust, from which they will profit. Some try to grind us into that self-doubt which believes our choices don't matter. But those are just forms of oppression and are not of God.

Why so many choices? Why so much free will? Why not just command and compel?

Because decisions are meaningless unless made freely, and because faith is meaningless unless attained and acted out freely. We cannot know who we are, who God is, or what our lives are about unless we have freedom to discern, to choose, to fail, and to try again.

The testing of Jesus in the wilderness was about choices. It wasn't about hunger, but about the dehumanizing, enslaving choices that evil laid before him. Would he remember his identity or not? Would he give in to easy satisfaction, easy wealth, easy power, or not? Would he take the casual path of accepting a false master, or not?

The testing makes no sense unless Jesus was free to make wrong choices. Why test him if his responses were preordained? What is there to admire in his answers if they weren't freely chosen?

Many readers have asked if I plan to see *The Passion of the Christ*. I am still deciding. I know I won't let my twelve-year-old son see it. A *Boston Globe* reviewer said, "Any parent who takes their child to see this movie is guilty of abuse." I don't particularly want to spend 126 minutes watching blood spatter.

I disagree with Mel Gibson's apparent belief that the suffering of Jesus is the heart of Christian faith. Being "saved by the blood of the Lamb" is too easy, too vicarious, too much a spectator faith, a consumable.

Yes, Jesus suffered for the choices he made. So, in ways small and large, do we all. The point is the quality of what we choose, not the gravity of the consequences. Do we choose love, God, kindness, peace, mercy, servanthood?

Or do we take the evil and easy way out? Do we know ourselves as children of God? Or accept evil's lies?

Sometimes, holy choices lead to pain, sometimes they lead to glory. We can't just measure the blood spatter. We must exercise more discernment and humility than that. Knowing that the wicked flayed Jesus' skin isn't as important as understanding why they did so.

QUESTION 58: "How do I recognize God speaking to me, and

does he always speak to everyone in the same ways?"

Jesus answered him, "It is said, 'Do not put the Lord your God to the test.'" When the devil had finished every test, he departed from him until an opportune time. (Luke 4:12–13)

I call a friend with two questions: Are we on for golf tomorrow? Is today a good day to pick up the bed he is giving us?

I need to listen carefully. Friends tend to be polite, not direct. Early-spring golf can be muddy and slow. Is he enthusiastic or grudging about the prospect? Enthusiastic, it seems, so we set a tee time.

Now, about the bed. He doesn't need it any longer, and we can use it in a spare bedroom. But does he really want to part with it? Is today truly a good day to come by with a truck? It isn't enough to recite Scripture, as it were. He offered the bed two months ago, but situations change. Today is a new day. I listen for hesitancy, hints of inconvenience. Hearing none, I say we will be over soon.

Am I being oversensitive? Maybe. But I know from experience that I need to work at listening. I tend to hear what I want to hear and to miss the rest. Better to confirm than to assume.

Listening for God is infinitely more difficult. It isn't enough to remember Scriptures, for God has much more to say than has ever been written down. God's word is living, restless, ever reaching.

It isn't enough to think on former things, for in God's creation new things are always bursting forth and must be attended. Yesterday's journey may contain signs, but today's requires fresh discernment.

It isn't enough to reflect on how God spoke to someone else, for each human heart has different needs and God a special word. Derivative faith never works. We must each take our own journey.

It isn't enough just to keep our ears open, for we are assaulted by noise, words, images, solicitations, and opportunities. Some come from the world, in varying degrees of malice or kindness, and must be sorted out. Some come from the evil power, who is probably more determined to ensnare us than we are to resist. Some come from God.

Which are which? Ah, the dilemma. The devil can quote Scripture as readily as Jesus can, so a stack of citations isn't sufficient. The devil can turn any fellowship or worship to corruption, so just holding hands and singing sweet songs aren't sufficient. We can't just follow the leader, because power is a prime opportunity for corruption, and godly authority requires more humility than most trained, chosen, and applauded leaders can muster.

Even after Jesus vanquished the devil in the wilderness, his opponent didn't surrender, but rather withdrew to await "an opportune time." Such as Peter's shallow confession and blustery insistence that messiah need not suffer. Such as the drawn sword in the garden of Gethsemane. Such as Pilate's offer of escape.

Life seems to be one "opportune time" after another. Evil is more like slow rot than grand theater. Give in a little here, take a little there; retreat into smugness here, dish out some unkindness there.

Most of us can't manage being eternally vigilant, so we require a healthy capacity for repentance. But casual confession falls short. We need to tend to our souls with the same attention to detail and awareness of consequences that we assign to, say, our checkbooks or our careers. Our choices, small as well as large, matter.

How, asks a reader, do we recognize God's voice? By working at it. Not in some derivative or weekly exercise, but in daily effort to discern for ourselves.

QUESTION 59: "Will you see and comment on *The Passion of the Christ*?"

[Jesus said,] "Jerusalem, Jerusalem, the city that kills the prophets and stones those who are sent to it!" (Luke 13:34)

I have decided not to see Mel Gibson's movie, *The Passion of the Christ.*

I don't question the sincerity of those who do see it and find it meaningful. But I am responsible for which images inform my consciousness. I choose not to imagine Jesus getting tortured to a bloody pulp without the larger context of his life.

I find it sad that, by clever advance publicity focused on the twin titillations of graphic violence and anti-Semitism, a niche film has become a box-office hit. I find it even sadder that, in a throwback to the Middle Ages, churches are using the film to evangelize, as if the Sermon on the Mount were nothing compared with the sight of blood.

I am not naive about cinema. I know films offer an odd slant on life. But I go into the theater knowing it is entertainment, that Michael Douglas is neither president nor wife murderer. My faith is a different matter. I have spent the past decade finding a Jesus who is livelier than the stale categories of inherited tradition, who touches life with a living word. At the risk of feeling an outsider, I peer into the gospels and pursue a journey that takes me far afield.

I don't wish to have that journey distorted by a 126-minute movie that reduces Jesus to penetrating images of blood and flesh and the shouting of a mob. I don't doubt that the torture occurred or that a mob of people like me found a murderer more appealing than a redeemer. But the story of Jesus is deeper and more disturbing than that.

Faith is largely a matter of yearning. It isn't proofs—documented evidence—and it isn't an appeal to base passions. Faith is a yearning to go home and yet to press on, a yearning to think the day worth living and yet worth sacrificing, a yearning for meaning and hope.

When the prophet went to Babylon to bid the Hebrews go home, he had a hard sell to make. They had been in exile too long. They had made their peace with Babylon and found a measure of comfort there. They were frightened of the desert.

Isaiah sang to the exiles' yearnings. He sang of Jerusalem. "Herald of good tidings," where those left behind would rejoice at the sight of returning exiles, where God's anointed would "feed his flock like a shepherd" (Isaiah 40:9, 11).

Yes, there was more to be said about Jerusalem, for it was corrupt, better as an ideal than as a reality. In the hands of avaricious kings, Jerusalem had too much pride, too much arrogance, too much prosperity. Some believed that the Hebrews should abandon Jerusalem, that they were never intended to be city dwellers.

When Jesus lamented over Jerusalem, he was keening an ancient woe. For this was indeed a city that killed prophets. He would be yet another victim of the powerful, the proud, those mired in self-serving religiosity.

But it takes the entirety of Jesus' life to understand that lamentation. It takes knowing that, when believers began to comprehend Jesus, they went instinctively to Isaiah's images, because at some level they knew themselves as exiles, as having made their peace with oppression, as having found comfort in the wrong place.

I know that yearning and see it in others. I don't see a hunger for blood, but for hope. I don't see a need to blame anyone for Jesus' death. I would rather hear Jesus weeping over a lost city—weeping over me and you—than bleeding in its streets. Not that the bleeding didn't occur, for it did. But the Stations of the Cross aren't the gospel in miniature. Jesus is revealed more fully elsewhere.

QUESTION 60: "How do we stop the division and pain on this earth even amongst your own community of believers? And are we wrong to be so weary of it all?"

[Jesus said,] "See, your house is left to you. And I tell you, you will not see me until the time comes when you say, 'Blessed is the one who comes in the name of the Lord.'" (Luke 13:35)

Rainy Saturday, a day spent indoors on writing projects. Time for a movie.

First choice: which movie? Weeding out R-rated flicks as inappropriate for our twelve-year-old son, we settle on *Starsky & Hutch*. Unlikely to be serious art, but entertaining.

Second choice: which theater, the handsome new theater south of town where moviegoing has an air of excitement, or the somewhat tattered theater closer to home?

The parking lot of our neighborhood cinema is one-third full. No line at the ticket window. Inside, we turn left to our destination screen, where a theater capable of seating 256 has 30 patrons. Is it the well-worn venue, superseded now by something glossier? Is it the film, not competing well at the box office with *The Passion* next door? Is it the Duke-Carolina game?

This, I think, is the reality of division within faith communities. People are making choices about faith, and that is troubling to those who think God laid out one path only. People who believe fervently in the absolute merit of their narrow gate are appalled when others choose different gates. In their mind, there are no choices, just a single-track truth. Take it or leave it.

In fact, people simply make choices. Those choices divide us, some going this direction and some that. Division, by itself, is neutral. Box-office boffo proves little. The pain comes when we engage in that spiritual triumphalism which says No to all choices but one's own.

A search for meaning must go deeper—deeper than the mere fact of division, deeper than counting the house, deeper than personal likes and dislikes, deeper than the shared convictions of people like oneself.

In the language of Jeremiah, Jesus warned the Pharisees that their house was desolate. But what did he mean by that? For in fact the temple in Jerusalem was as lively as ever, filled with people, a safe haven for Hebrews amid Roman oppression. If you measured the crowd, the temple was a hit.

Desolation, it seems, wasn't to be measured by numbers. Or, if you read on in the Gospels, by adherence to inherited tradition, or by overt religiosity, or by toeing the Mosaic line, or by claiming tribe or party, or by saying the right words.

Jesus gave people choices. That was one consequence of his teaching in parables. That's why the no-choice crowd always teaches laws, not stories. That's why the early church was built on Paul—or an absolutist reading of Paul—and not on the Gospels.

Jesus issued invitations, not commands. "Come and see," he said, not, "Do this or die." Compulsion isn't adequate ground for faith. Neither is groupthink.

Faith is a turning of the whole person to the light. It happens gradually, in fits and starts, and the last bit of turning probably falls to God's gracious hands. Desolation is a refusal to start turning. The spiritual bankruptcy of the Pharisees wasn't wrong opinion, antiquated beliefs, tribal identity, or even excessive zeal for privilege and wealth. Their home was desolate because they had closed their minds and stopped turning.

That, in my opinion, is the "pain," as a reader puts it, of today's "division." Not the fact of division, for division is neutral, but that cruel absolutism, born of insecurity and pride, which would demean or punish others for making different choices.

God can deal with bad choices. Look at Peter. But a closed mind leads to desolation.

QUESTION 61: "How can I get closer to you?"

[Jesus said, "The younger son] set off and went to his father. But while he was still far off, his father saw him and was filled with compassion; he ran and put his arms around him and kissed him."
(Luke 15:20)

I am sitting at a departure gate, waiting to put my twelve-year-old son onto his first transcontinental flight. He will be retrieved 3,000 miles later by his uncle.

I am nervous. It is no small thing to put a child onto an airplane, to start him on a journey of many miles, a journey farther into maturity. He will be changed by this trip. Seeing new places, spending a weekend with another family, traveling by himself, and having internal adventures beyond my imagining will bring him home a new boy.

I try to imagine what the father in Jesus' parable felt when his son went away. Did he already know his son was weak, a wastrel in the making? Did he see the grabbing of inheritance for what it was? Did he imagine the best, the worst? Did he lie awake nights?

I picture him as sorrowful. Not sorry to see the child become a man, for that is a necessary journey, but sorry to see critical stages in that journey happening beyond his sight, on shaky ground, beyond his capacity to help. Maybe he wondered what his son was experiencing. Maybe he just missed him.

When I pick up my son on Monday, I will be looking for his face. Not a report card on how he behaved, not an account of his adventures, not his learnings or frustrations. Those will come in time. But first I will look for his face, the sight of him drawing near. That will be my joy.

I wonder if we could ever understand God in that way? As compassionate, as so eager to see us that God runs and embraces. That is how Jesus portrays God in his parable. That is how Jesus treated people. I believe that is how Jesus expects us to treat one another.

Not the scorekeeping God proclaimed by those who love rules and punishments. Not the grudge-holding God of those who cannot forgive. Not the controlling God who determines all things. Not the triumphalist God who sees the sinner repenting and shouts, "Gotcha!" Not any of those faces of God that have been lifted up over the centuries by the angry, unforgiving, controlling, legalistic, and frightened.

Jesus proclaimed a God who yearns for the sight of us, who is so thrilled at seeing us draw near that, abandoning the prerogatives of the indignant parent, God sees us from far away and rushes to greet us.

How did we ever get so wasteful of God that we proclaimed God as little more than an extension of ourselves? Judgmental, in the way we dismiss and disparage. Score-minded, in the way we track every failing of others. Harsh, in the way we are cold. Legalistic, in the way we want to control the calculus of grace.

Who would want to go home to a God like that? A reader asks how she can get closer to God. The first step is to imagine God as wanting her close. The second is to start moving. The third is to see God's smile and outstretched arms, and to run into those arms, not in defeat, not in humiliation, not in any return to the smallness of childhood, but in gladness—in God's gladness and in her own.

Our religious world is awash in harsh images of God. Mean and spiteful. Cold and distanced. The worst of fathers, the worst of mothers. Enough of that! To build their franchises, religions might portray a God who loves conditionally. But Jesus spoke of a God who never ceases to scan the horizon, looking for our return.

QUESTION 62: "Why is it so hard to love God? Why am I, after all these years, still so much in my own way most of the time?"

[Jesus said,] "The father said to his slaves, 'Quickly, bring out a

robe—the best one—and put it on him; put a ring on his finger and
sandals on his feet. And get the fatted calf and kill it, and let us eat
and celebrate; for this son of mine was dead and is alive again; he
was lost and is found!'" (Luke 15:22–24)

As my twelve-year-old son makes his way to the West Coast, I receive
several updates by cell phone.

He reports safe arrival at his first stop, then reports equipment
problems ("a hole in the plane") and a delay. When he asks an airline
clerk for information, she sounds distracted. We agree he should stay
near the check-in desk.

His next call has him being escorted to another gate. He sounds
worried and surrounded by commotion. He reports again with news of
more delay.

The next time my cell phone rings, however, my son sounds relaxed.
The airline has taken him to a "young travelers club," where he has
snacks, movies, and comfortable chairs. An attendant says they are keeping his uncle informed about pickup time. Later, the airline calls with
updated times. Three hours late, but intact, my son reports safe arrival.

I am amazed at the airline's extra mile of caring. Why am I amazed?
I have paid dearly for this service, but seasoned travelers expect little for
their travel dollar. A paid-for ticket seems more like an ante in poker
than a guarantee of service.

A reader asks why it is hard for her to love God. I think immediately
of my low expectations of an airline.

Over the years, believers have allowed God to become small, narrow,
harsh, and mean. They claim to have scriptural justification; they
certainly have institutional imperatives, for time-tested ways to build
loyalty to an institution include frightening people and appealing
to their insecurity, need for superiority, ethnic or class pride, and
self-loathing. By portraying God as small and partisan, institutions can
claim the moral and spiritual high ground in the competition for market share.

But how can one love a God who is so small, so calculating in
dispensing favors, so insistent on our toeing the line? One can fear such
a God, maybe even obey. But love requires more.

In his parable of the prodigal son, Jesus portrays God as extravagant
in compassion, kindness, generosity, forgiveness, and joy. To the elder
son's dismay, the father goes overboard in welcoming the wastrel with
robe, ring, food, and celebration—way beyond the typical images of
God as parsimonious in giving and reluctant in mercy.

To love God, one must see God as loving. And not just loving in the normal human way, but loving beyond measure, beyond self-interest, beyond reason. To submit to God, we must trust God's compassion. To draw near to God, we must believe in God's welcome. For any of that to happen, we must stop needing God to be so small.

I realize that life is confusing. Modernity has much that is distasteful, moral issues are puzzling, society's tolerance might exceed our own, and the more we see of human diversity, the less sure we are of ourselves. But the answer to such confusion isn't to make God small or partisan or angry or merciless.

If we require God to be that small, we will never have a meaningful relationship with God. We might find a like-minded fellowship and feel temporarily safe, but we won't know God. For God isn't like that. God looks for our return and is extravagant in welcoming us home.

Such a welcome will be amazing—more amazing than an airline's extra caring.

QUESTION 63: "Will you save everyone?"

[Jesus said,] "Then the father said to [the elder brother], 'Son, you are always with me, and all that is mine is yours. But we had to celebrate and rejoice, because this brother of yours was dead and has come to life; he was lost and has been found.'" (Luke 15:31–32)

I don't expect to win our office pool in college basketball's national championships. My goal is modest: not to come in last again.

So far, so good. As of Saturday night, I am third from last. It looks promising for Monday morning rehashing. One of our local teams is still alive; another plays today and is favored. If Kentucky will just lose, all will be right with the world of basketball.

Spoken, of course, like a true fan. For beyond peewee league, sports is about winning and losing. The college tourney starts with sixty-four teams and relentlessly eliminates all but one. It is a mirror of life. The hallways of life are littered with the dashed dreams of those who didn't make cheerleader, didn't get the job, didn't make the sale, couldn't afford their dream house.

For my team to win, everyone else must lose. It is fine to give every child a prize at the soccer banquet, but out there, where only the fittest survive, everyone recognizes such softness for what it is: a denial of reality.

Or so the story goes, shaping expectations and making sports perhaps our primary metaphor for life.

It certainly has become our metaphor for salvation. Some win, some lose. Winning goes to those who join the right team (Christianity), practice hard (religion), overcome adversity (evil), follow the rules (good), and listen to the coach (God). All others lose.

We disagree over who belongs on the team, but rarely do we doubt that our team will win.

The idea that Muslims might have equal access to God is bizarre to many Christians. How could that possibly be? What about the "narrow gate"? If God plays no favorites, what is the point of belonging? If anyone can enter heaven, why obey the rules? If the game doesn't reward winners, why try?

A reader asks, Will God save everyone? I certainly hope so.

If any of the common metaphors for salvation is true—sports, warfare, competitive romance, academic tenure—then I am doomed. So are we all. For in the end, we all lose. Our prowess might be strong now, but teams change, skills fade, and next season might be a disaster. Winning one war just sets the stage for the next. None of us can remain young forever. Someone always knows more. Wal-Mart will follow Woolworth onto the slag heap of history.

On its own evidence, life is pessimistic. Things wind down. If we learned nothing else last century, with its wars, depression, Holocaust, and nuclear terror, fairness is a conceit of the temporarily successful. To link God with such momentary fairness is a cruel pathway to despair.

Our hope doesn't lie in victory, not even in those victories associated with religion. Our hope lies in the mercy and grace of God. Not when God applies the standards that we would apply, or when God parcels out rewards and punishment as we imagine fairness would dictate, but when God is God, when God does what God wants to do, when God loves all that God has made, when God sees the sinner afar off and rushes to greet him, when God takes the side of the harlot, when God touches the leper, when God feeds everyone, even the betrayer, and when God looks with tenderness on humanity.

We wouldn't behave that way. We would be more like the elder son, applying more rigorous standards, always separating sheep from goat and feeling justified in doing so. But we aren't God. The elder son doesn't determine the father's love.

Chapter 6

Peace

QUESTION 64: "I find it increasingly difficult to believe in a compassionate God when there seems to be no reachable peace on earth. I would ask God why he doesn't work on people's hearts so that they can love instead of hate, seek peace instead of war."

In the fifteenth year of the reign of Emperor Tiberius, when Pontius Pilate was governor of Judea, and Herod was ruler of Galilee, and his brother Philip ruler of the region of Ituraea and Trachonitis, and Lysanias ruler of Abilene. . . . (Luke 3:1)

My golfing partner and I are tied coming to the final hole. Our play is better than yesterday, but still inadequate. Tomorrow looms: back to work, Christmas shopping, seasonal insanity.

Despite all this, we walk through a gorgeous day, and I am overwhelmed by a feeling of peace. "This is good," I say.

Peace is fleeting—I am gnashing my teeth minutes later after depositing a shot in a lake. Peace is far from universal—while we golf, bloodshed continues in Iraq and down the street.

Why, after all this time, does warfare still rule human affairs? Long ago, John the Baptist proclaimed return from exile and said that "all flesh shall see the salvation of God." A woman named Mary told of the night her son was born and angels sang of "peace on earth." And yet peace remains elusive.

Of all the questions that readers asked, peace was the most common topic. One wrote of political leaders too "spineless" to resist warfare and churches too caught up in "religiosity and bureaucracy" to make a difference. A reader being brutalized by a greedy congregation asked, "Why are humans so awful to each other?" A reader whose denomination is fracturing asked, "Can you teach us how to live in harmony?" Several readers yearned for "the peace, contentment, and joy of living I had as a child."

These are more than "woe is me" questions, more than partisanship wondering whom to blame. They cut to the heart of faith. Why is God so seemingly helpless? Why does God not deliver on Christmas promises? If we sing of peace but return to war, what does that say about the rest of our hymns and prayers? Are they equally futile?

When you cut through the partisan slants, the same question tends to emerge: Why doesn't God fix things?

One answer, of course, has to do with freedom. God has left us free to choose life or death, blessing or curse. We can get along or get a gun. The only lasting peace occurs when we rise above hubris, find better ways to express fear, master our bloodlust, and give up our triumphal claims. But the question remains: what is God doing to help us make better choices?

One clue lies in the way Luke told the story of John's appearance, followed soon by Jesus' appearance. He grounded it in historical time— the era of Emperor Tiberius—and named the rulers whose decisions shaped behavior. But these rulers were merely a backdrop to the story.

Whatever God intended through John and Jesus had nothing to do with changing the hearts of Tiberius, Pontius Pilate, Herod, Philip, or Lysanias.

Our venue for discerning peace or war, fulfillment or abandonment, hope or despair apparently isn't the large stage where affairs of state are determined. That is the realm of power, greed, and control—sometimes exercised with grace, more often not. There power corrupts, and the outcome tends to be warfare.

God, it seems, works a different venue, closer to home, closer to life as we actually live it. It was no accident that messiah and herald came to common folk, not to the grand. God's working for peace happens far from the throne of worldly power.

God's peace isn't the absence of war headlines from Baghdad. God's peace is one soul laying down sword and shield.

QUESTION 65: "What do we most need for peace to come in our world? What sacrifices are needed, and who needs to make them?"

[Mary said,] "*He has brought down the powerful from their thrones, and lifted up the lowly; he has filled the hungry with good things, and sent the rich away empty.*" (Luke 1:52–53)

Shopping venues seem unusually calm on this Friday before Christmas.

A once-thriving retail center near my office is empty. Store owners gaze bleakly at doors through which no one is passing. Even at a "big box" mall featuring Wal-Mart and Best Buy, parking is available, and checkout lines are short. Where is everyone?

I don't object. But I do wonder. Are people waiting longer, shopping elsewhere, or not buying as much? Because of the intricate web that ties my economic well-being to other people's personal spending, a shortfall in Christmas sales will eventually hit home.

If people are shopping elsewhere, this mall will tailspin, a travel corridor will deteriorate, and my house near that corridor won't appreciate in value. If my neighbors spend less, my company could find our consulting services harder to sell.

In a complex system all parts are interrelated. A slight twitch in DVD sales will cause tremors elsewhere. Advertisers who say, "Buy more, you'll feel better," and preachers who say, "Buy less, you'll feel better," are both playing with fire. If enough people bake cookies and forgo shopping, jobs will be lost and some will suffer.

Determining who suffers has become the heart of our political-economic system. Will it be the rich, middle class, or poor? Democrats in New York or Republicans in Texas? The elderly or young? Whose jobs will be lost? Whose houses won't sell? Whose infrastructure will crumble?

This is a complex mix of public policy, political gamesmanship, corporate strategy, and cascading individual choices, all of it confusing, even to the experts.

The biblical epoch doesn't seem to have been this complicated. Systems for allocating power and wealth were relatively simple. A poet writing in the late Bronze Age could talk of her God bringing down the mighty and raising up the lowly, because that is the way her world worked. Tribes made war, and the victor redistributed wealth.

When Mary used Hannah's poem, we can sense how little the world had changed between 1100 B.C. and the apostolic era. But vast sea changes have occurred since then. Nations replaced empires. Land-based economies gave way to trading economies, then to industrial, and now to a complex global economy in which a permanent underclass makes the goods, city-states like New York and Shanghai trade the goods, knowledge workers run the system, and a tiny ownership class gets extraordinarily rich.

How you feel about that system depends partly on your place in it. What you can do about it seems limited. You can make better moral choices in your personal life, but the systemic impacts of those choices will be difficult to discern and could be self-defeating. Less shopping, for example, could hurt your retirement savings.

What, then, is the answer to the reader's question about peace? I assume he means warfare, hostilities between classes and among nations—the consequences, in other words, of how political-economic systems allocate power and wealth.

We can imagine Hannah's ancient vision coming true—winners and losers trading places—but peace seems to flow from justice, not from victory in war. Justice seems to flow from equitable distribution of wealth and hope. Equitable distribution seems to flow from cascading individual decisions not to demand a lot more than the next person. Those individual decisions seem to flow from faith—a faith that locates hope and meaning in the grace of God, not in wealth and power.

In my opinion, the Christian movement needs to stop fighting over right opinion on fringe issues, and to wade where Jesus waded—into the realities of wealth and power, as confusing as they have become.

QUESTION 66: "What do we most need for peace to come in our world? What sacrifices are needed, and who needs to make them?"

At that very hour some Pharisees came and said to [Jesus], "Get away from here, for Herod wants to kill you." (Luke 13:31)

Time to buy my son soccer cleats and shorts. Time for my annual question: Is this the year they learn teamwork?

All things seem possible when trying on shiny Adidas shoes.

Coaches say teamwork comes with maturity. I'd say the opposite is true: that maturity comes with learning teamwork. Either way, there does come a time—for some—when passing the ball wins games, sacrifice matters more than stardom, and thanking one's teammates when accepting applause is sincere.

I will not be surprised, however, if this team practices shooting more than passing, and assigns the most talented to offense, where they will hog the ball, doting parents will shriek their names, and the no-names on defense will actually determine outcomes. I wish more could learn in sports what I learned in choral music: real joy comes from self-sacrificial teamwork.

Age by itself isn't enough. It takes coaching and hard lessons. A local university, for example, has arguably the most talented starting lineup in college basketball. But they are mired in mediocrity because coddled stars won't play as a team. Too much adulation has made them soft. My answer: encourage the glitter boys to turn pro and let the coach recruit team players with grit.

A reader asks what it will take for peace to come in our world. Maybe we should start by learning teamwork and sacrifice. And by learning to discern their opposites.

Luke tells of the Pharisees warning Jesus of Herod's murderous intent. What was actually going on? Imagine a youth shouting, "Pass me the ball!" as if he were encouraging teamwork, when in fact he just wants the ball.

The Pharisees had made their peace with Roman oppressors. By not threatening the political establishment, they were allowed to be the religious establishment. They wore fine clothes, took honored seats, and deployed religion to exercise control.

When they warned Jesus of Herod's rage, their intent probably was to get this meddlesome messiah out of town. To protect their franchise, they wanted Jesus gone. Their warning wasn't in his interest, but their own. Jesus saw through their hypocrisy and lamented the faithlessness of Jerusalem's temple cult.

Peace is a difficult matter; for some, violence is truly righteous. A parent will defend a child with whatever weapons are at hand, and rightfully so. Some revolutions need to happen, some self-defense is worthy, some battles against oppressors are necessary. Violence rarely resolves conflict, for violence tends to beget more violence, but oppression and degradation also are self-replicating until the cycle is broken.

But most violence proves to have a seamy core, a dirty little secret of self-interest run amok. Profiteers turn up in every war and discourage efforts toward peace. Every oppressor finds cooperative theologians hungry for privilege. Wars tend to be about land, class, and race, not the noble cause carried as standard, and their leaders tend to have more hubris than vision.

Young men and women die when the powerful shout for the ball and sound so sincere. We need to be wary of them, as Jesus was of the Pharisees, and more discerning of true intent. It may have been Caesar's minions who executed Jesus, but it was his own people, entourage, and disciples who were most offended by him and betrayed him. For they hadn't yet attained that maturity which enables one to live for others, not for self. Jesus' call to self-sacrifice fell on proud ears.

Our path to peace, therefore, probably starts in learning to distinguish ball hog from team player, to count teamwork higher than adulation, and to understand that self-sacrifice is a far better coach than self-interest.

QUESTION 67: "I would ask God why he doesn't work on people's hearts so that they can love instead of hate, and seek peace instead of war."

[Jesus said,] "Yet today, tomorrow, and the next day I must be on my way, because it is impossible for a prophet to be killed outside of Jerusalem." (Luke 13:33)

"What is it like playing the violin?" I ask my twelve-year-old son as we drive to school.

He speaks poetically about the miracle of music, of seeing notes on a page and converting them into sound. "When I play, I feel at peace."

Does articulating such joys cause him to take violin in hand tonight? No, of course not. He shoots baskets and does homework, but I hear not a sound from the violin realm.

There is a disconnect here, the same disconnect that complicates life for most of us. He sees a joy but doesn't connect it to an action. He treasures the consequences of practice and knows where they came from, but doesn't take up his bow.

His heart isn't the issue. Nor is his will, for he is diligent. The issue is integrating the connection between outcome and behavior. Imposing habit or schedule just masks the dilemma, resolving it in one room but leaving it unchecked in another.

A habit of prayer, for example, doesn't make one's next decision wise or holy. The faithful are as prone to hateful behavior as others.

One answer to the reader's question, you see, is that God does "work on people's hearts," but that isn't enough. God also works on people's minds, enabling us to connect the dots of experience and to recognize the futility of hatred and warfare. But that isn't enough, either. We have all the data we need, from Moses to Isaiah to Jesus to the history of our violent orb. We know reality, and we feel it, as well.

What's missing is the connection, the integrated link between yearning and behavior. That missing link might be the greatest mystery about our human lot. We know, we feel, and yet we still foul our own nest and others.

That is why God's walk with us is ultimately a sorrowful journey, and our ultimate image of God needs to be not one who shows us the right path or fixes us, but one who weeps over us and agrees to bear such sorrow.

Jesus spoke with sad irony when he told the Pharisees that he must leave Jerusalem in order to stay alive. For the heart of his people's faith was corrupt. The holy city that God intended to be a beacon to the nations had chosen to walk in darkness. The city to which God had sent prophet after prophet—whose songs, lamentations, and visions formed the very core of faith—was also the city that "stones those who are sent to it."

Jesus didn't lay a curse on Jerusalem, or launch an evangelistic campaign to "save" Jerusalem, or build a Jesus reminder on every corner, or write new laws for a wayward people. He wept over the city, as he wept over Lazarus. He accepted the deep sorrow of one who loves and yet loses. He made the connection between mind and heart, between actual and ideal, between experience and vision—and that connection broke his heart.

We want God to be a fixer, a strong ruler who makes things right, a teacher who shows us the right way. But what we probably need to know is God's sorrow. We need to hear the sound of God walking in the garden, crying out for his beloved, and from that sorrow producing a music that tears at our souls.

Until we hear that mournful requiem and join its symphony of sorrow, we will continue to want peace but to make war, to yearn for love but to sow hatred.

Chapter 7

Evil

QUESTION 68: "How can we deal with evil without being infected by it?"

Jesus, filled with the power of the Spirit, returned to Galilee, and a report about him spread through all the surrounding country. He began to teach in their synagogues and was praised by everyone. (Luke 4:14–15)

Four Democratic presidential contenders will find out today who, in the opinion of Iowans, is the most popular. Or best suited to leadership. Or possessed of compelling ideas. Or the least unsavory. Or the best dresser.

In all likelihood, the message from Iowa won't be clear. So they will trudge on to New Hampshire and then head south, each hoping to seize momentum and to emerge as consensus favorite. Other politicians are on the road, too, hoping that the favorites will stub their toes, collapse in the polls, and create an opening.

In a large, diverse, and largely distracted democracy, election results are hard to read. How each candidate would lead remains a mystery, because stating vision, ideas, solutions, and questions has little place in modern elections. Any candidate who shows the intellectual capacity to see multiple viewpoints and the humility to embrace doubt can count on being seen as weak. It is easier, safer, and more cost-effective to manage image and to hope that no one gets too close to one's core reality. Stay on message, say the consultants.

Instead of listening to voters—which admittedly would be an enormous task—candidates measure their own ability to create impact.

If the crowd is cheering, that is all they need to know. Nuances within the cheers—yearnings, passions, hatreds, evil desires—don't interest them. Just count and measure at the macro level.

Jesus faced exactly this dilemma. For the evil one tested him in four ways. First was their one-on-one duel in the wilderness, where Satan offered Jesus every despot's dream package: easy ascent to power, unlimited wealth and grandeur. Second was the adulation of the crowd, that intoxicating roar of approval which has driven many a leader insane. Third was when his disciples tried to engage Jesus in their own vainglory. Fourth was offering a way out of ultimate suffering.

A reader asks how to "deal with evil without being infected by it." The answer lies in wrestling with these four temptations: power, approval, pride, and safety. They come from different directions, each has its own seduction, each sounds plausible, and yet each has but one aim: to distort the self.

In this season of cheering—presidential politics, professional football, college basketball, plus all the small ways we try to seduce one another with applause—we might start by examining how Jesus responded to applause.

Crowd buzz began immediately. Before he did much of anything, he was "praised by everyone." Had people heard his message and been moved by it? Not at all. They were in love with their own enthusiasm.

Modern politicians, like self-serving leaders of all ages, know how to manipulate that adulation and to ride its crest to greater power and glory. "I have a mandate!" they shout. What did Jesus do? He went immediately to his home synagogue and told them the truth about who he was and what he had come to do.

They hated him for it. They tried to kill him. For his message wasn't at all the message they wanted to project onto him. He saw them as they were trying not to see themselves. He saw an urgency that they were hoping to avoid. He presented God in ways that offended the tame God-of-convenience that they had spent centuries developing.

That became Jesus' pattern. Just as he dealt with Satan's promise of easy power by remembering the truth about God, he dealt with applause by telling the truth about himself. He wanted followers, but their following had to be grounded in who he was, not in what they wanted him to be.

QUESTION 69: "Why the depravity of the human heart? And if our sin is permitted as an act of free will given to us out of love, then how can sin and evil be vanquished?"

The devil led [Jesus] up and showed him in an instant all the king-doms of the world. And the devil said to him, "To you I will give their glory and all this authority; for it has been given over to me, and I will give it to anyone I please. If you, then, will worship me, it will all be yours." (Luke 4:5–7)

My son tells me about a fight at middle school, the latest in a string of fights between whites and blacks.

This one involved two top students and apparently stemmed from a perceived insult. The boys went straight for each other's heads, pounding and slapping. Both were suspended. The white boy was bereft at losing to a black. Neither boy, my son says, views suspension as an issue, since they have bedrooms filled with entertainment gear, and parents who don't care.

Can we count the lies at work here?

Lie: that violence solves anything. Lie: that hurting another person builds up oneself. Lie: that suspension will correct behavior. Lie: that one's standing as a person is defined by racial superiority. Lie: that a day pleasantly spent is adequate preparation for life. Lie: that children can raise themselves.

Who spun this web of deceit? No one person, no one cultural force. Lies about race are deeply embedded in the human psyche. To understand casual violence, you would have to peer into the boys' homes and what they see on television. To understand disregard for consequences, you would have to study our reality-denying culture. To understand parenting today, you would have to study the collapse of families.

No one lie explains it all. No one perpetrator of lies takes all blame. It is a web, a blanket of falsehood, that silently envelopes us and makes us feel safe. My son's class is studying World War II and how Hitler convinced a civilized nation to become monsters. He did it with lies, buttressed by propaganda, always plausible and uplifting.

Can you count the lies that Satan told Jesus? That he intended to give Jesus glory and power, that sovereignty had been granted to him, that he would share his sovereignty with Jesus in exchange for fealty, that he had Jesus' interests at heart. This is how evil works: promising what it cannot deliver, promising what we want to receive, promising to care steadfastly, promising anything in exchange for accepting corruption.

It isn't one big lie, one take-it-or-leave-it falsehood that we suspend all judgment to accept. It is a promise here, an insinuation there, a phony but plausible invitation, an easy excuse, a casual cruelty that is named normal, a diversion of attention onto the trivial, a distortion of the good, a lure of escape, an edge of control. We accept this blanket because we are fundamentally cold and needy. Evil seems reasonable—more reasonable, in fact, than reality itself. Liars rarely are the leering, ugly ogres of medieval art. They are smooth, friendly, seemingly kind, and what they offer often seems more inviting, certainly easier, than what goodness offers.

How do we "vanquish" sin and evil? Not by ourselves, not overnight, not without considerable effort, not without having to make the very choices that we tend to resist. A single act—baptism, major confession, epic contrition—won't do it. Neither will a grandiose "never again." Evil is too clever and too determined. Vanquishing evil requires that we have some sense of the good—not the bigotry and narrow-mindedness that religious zealots sell as the good, but goodness itself, as lived by Jesus. And it requires one choice, and then another, and another, in a cycle that never stops, against an assault that never ends.

Chapter 8

Relationship

QUESTION 70: "I would ask God to show me how to let go of my fear/reluctance to reach out to another human when I'm in need of comfort. I can be there for another, but I can't seem to let them get close to me."

John answered all of them by saying, "I baptize you with water; but one who is more powerful than I is coming; I am not worthy to untie the thong of his sandals." (Luke 3:16)

Getting close is what this weekend is about.

As my mother gets close to dying time, the family gathers to get close to her, to Dad, and to one another.

Getting close means hugs at the airport, laughter while driving, serious sibling talk about what is happening with our parents, hugs at home, trying to read the moment, talking openly about funeral plans, taking a walk with my brother, talking about houses and children, a family meal, and a family chat.

Getting close is physical—touching, sitting in one room, walking side by side. Getting close is words—speaking and listening, taking turns, allowing room for anything that needs to be said.

Getting close has nothing to do with expertise or getting it right. This isn't a performance being measured, but a journey being shared. We will all try to do and say loving things. That is enough to know. If we stumble in funeral planning, so be it. If our words come out wrong, so be it.

We aren't adding the final layer of paint to a portrait, with the risk of ruining the final product. We are walking to the corner, crossing the street here, maybe there, saying whatever seems right to say, buying eggnog, and returning home. We won't mess up our family's history by missing a beat. We won't perfect the story by polishing the final chapter.

John the Baptist knew two things: he had a potent ministry, and he wasn't messiah. That cut two ways. On the one hand, he had power, capability, commanding presence—but he wasn't the Son of God. He needed to get his potency into perspective. On the other hand, he wasn't messiah, but he still had potency, still had a responsibility to serve as best he could.

I think the perfectionist tendencies of religion serve us poorly. From wanting to prepare the altar perfectly to demanding perfect perform- ance of clergy, from laboring over budgets to laboring over doctrine, from preparing precisely worded mission statements to dissecting passages of Scripture, we worry too much about error and measure ourselves too much by a standard of perfection.

Those same perfectionist tendencies hold us back in the rest of life. Many are worrying about buying perfect Christmas gifts. Many are worrying about year-end performance evaluations, family and business budgeting, college entrance exams, and first-semester grades.

It is good to try our best and to hold ourselves to high standards. But at some point, we need to join John the Baptist in recognizing that none of us is God, none of us is perfect, and yet each of us has merit and potency. That means a humble submission to God, both a submission to God's sovereignty and a submission to God's confidence in us.

I don't know specifically what blocks this reader from getting close to others. But in my experience, the obstacle usually has to do with fear of failure, fear of being known, fear of rejection, and fear of losing control.

God's answer to those fears hasn't been to explain perfection more carefully, or to encourage perfection by punishing failure, or to send messengers to name winners and losers, or to offer foolproof tech- niques.

God's answer has been mercy, compassion, steadfastness, and trust. Even as his disciples erred and strayed, Jesus kept walking forward with them, showing them that life isn't a scorecard but a journey, and you do the best you can.

QUESTION 71: "Given the opportunity, I would ask Jesus to help me know what it feels like to be loved unconditionally, and to recognize and accept that love."

He was in the world, and the world came into being through him; yet the world did not know him. He came to what was his own, and his own people did not accept him. (John 1:10–11)

I can tell this reader what it feels like to be "loved unconditionally." It feels thrilling and chastening.

Thrilling, to open a Christmas gift and to sense that the giver knows me fully, not just my wish list and proper size, but my person and what delights me. Chastening, to wonder if I have given that same depth of knowing in return. I tried, but I sense that I fell short.

It feels warm and challenging. Warm, to be surrounded by love that asks nothing in return. Challenging, to have no road map for giving back, for if nothing is asked in return, how do I know what to give?

It feels freeing and compelling. Freeing, to know that for this instant I can just be myself—not need to please or to perform. Compelling, to step beyond expectations but not know where to step next: set up boundaries? keep going? create expectations even where none exist?

It feels joyful and sad. Joyful, to be lifted up by another's regard. Sad, to know time's restless churning, to know that this moment will end.

Being loved is exhausting. That is how I end this Christmas Day: exhausted. Depleted from my small share in meal preparation, but even more, humbled by others who give the larger share. Pleased to watch my sons love each other and a romance taking further shape, but also drained by observing the swirling ballet and by knowing that it is now up to them, that there is little I can do to strengthen their bonds or to tutor their romance.

Being loved means encountering one's fundamental otherness. The more I love my wife and children, the more I see them as their own persons, not as extensions of me, and in that otherness, they think thoughts that aren't about me, but have an autonomy that is mine to appreciate but not to shape or to diminish.

It would be much easier if love were a transaction like other transactions. Count the cost, set boundaries to preserve self, pull back when fair measure isn't given in return. Match need for need, but don't look deeply into eyes that burn with delight. Ask where a touch is going, but don't just allow a caress to occur.

If we learn anything from our own experiences of loving and being loved, we should know exactly why Jesus came to his own and his own rejected him, and why that is the archetype for life writ broadly. It is frightening to be loved as Jesus loved. No wonder they thought him mad. No wonder they tried to disempower him with titles, legalism, the boundary-walking power of intellect.

They kept pushing him to name the payoff, because they couldn't imagine love without cost and benefit. They kept pushing him to declare some people outside the sheepfold, because they couldn't imagine arms wider than theirs. To this day, Christians are obsessed with payoffs, boundaries, who's in and who's out. We think we are protecting God with our rules and doctrines, when in fact we are only concerned with protecting ourselves.

What does it feel like to recognize and to accept God's unconditional love? It feels like letting go of such pretense, such self-protection. It means living as dangerously as we know how to live, which is out in the open, beyond the sheltering bulwarks of self, beyond the comforts of measurement and exchange.

It means opening a gift and having nothing to say but, "Thank you."

QUESTION 72: "I loved my father. He was a good man, a simple man of few words, a wise man. When he smiled on me or when he'd clap me on the shoulder or tussle my head and hair, it felt like the sun shining upon me. I was his and he was proud of me. I didn't have to be perfect, I wasn't. It didn't matter. He loved me. That's what I'd like to have with Jesus."

Joseph got up, took the child and his mother by night, and went to Egypt, and remained there until the death of Herod. This was to fulfill . . . the prophet, "Out of Egypt I have called my son." (Matthew 2:14–15)

I am a father, a son, and a husband. New Year's Eve finds me wanting to be protective on all fronts.

Tonight, my three sons will be out on the town. I don't know my older boys' plans, but I pray for them anyway, that they will avoid mayhem and make wise decisions.

My twelve-year-old son's plans sound harmless enough, but I know that now is when temptations emerge. I pray for his safety.

Six hundred miles away, my parents will be apart this evening: my mother in a hospice unit, my father home alone. Dad and I will talk, and I will wish I could make everything better.

My wife and I will have a quiet evening at home, our first New Year's Eve in this new house, a time to celebrate our blessings. Life hasn't been simple for us. But we have survived. We have been to

"Egypt" more than once and have come out of it stronger each time.

Fathers, sons, and husbands cannot always protect their families from harm. Accidents happen, illness and death are relentless, careers get squirrelly, the world is a confusing and dangerous place, we often undermine our good intentions, and sustaining a family is challenging work. We do the best we can, but our best often seems insufficient.

Safety certainly is temporary. Joseph took Mary and Jesus out of harm's way for a time, but only long enough for Jesus to grow up and to face life on his own. In the end, neither Joseph nor Mary could protect Jesus from suffering. Nor would they have wanted to shield him, for suffering was his destiny.

Besides, lifetime protection from harm isn't any father's gift to a child. The gift that counts is love. A reader remembers his father as "sun shining" in his life. At our best, we send our children forth knowing they are loved. On that foundation, they can face life and learn to love others. They can believe in God. They can make their world a better place— suffering on behalf of others, healing life's inevitable wounds and injustices, passing on to their partners and offspring what they received.

Joseph, a mystery man in many respects, was a steadfast partner to Mary, protected his family at their most vulnerable, responded to God's direction, and taught his son a trade. I suspect that, together, he and Mary taught their son to love.

It is difficult to take as a role model a biblical character who is so sparingly described. Perhaps it is enough to know that, when danger loomed, Joseph acted. I believe that the bottom line for grownups is to protect children, for partners to protect each other, and for grown children to protect their parents. That means recognizing danger, taking action as best one can, and remaining attentive as long as danger remains.

Love, you see, is more than a dreamy attitude. Love is action. Love lays down its own life for the good of the other. The man asking this question remembers the sunshine moments, but I imagine he knows, as we all know, that his father's sun tamed storms and darkness.

QUESTION 73: "What does it take for a broken heart to heal? Why does love outweigh common sense? Why is it so hard to move on from a relationship where trust was broken again and again?"

[Joseph] made his home in a town called Nazareth, so that what had been spoken through the prophets might be fulfilled, "He will be called a Nazorean." (Matthew 2:23)

"I guess break is coming to an end," says my twelve-year-old son, as he tackles a project that could have been started two weeks ago.

Break is also ending for those who saw Christmas and New Year's Day falling on Thursdays and joined schoolchildren in extended time off.

Tomorrow classes and workplaces resume regular schedules, alarm clocks get set, rush-hour traffic reclaims the road, and intricate scheduling recommences.

For some this is a happy day; for others tomorrow is the real "winter solstice," when time seems to stand still and onward means a gauntlet of pipers lining up for payment. For some Christmas has been a pleasant interlude; for others extra work and too much grieving.

The challenge is to realize that around us are people having different experiences of the same moment. Those who welcome resumption of regular life need to know that others find their regular lives horrible or boring. Those who dread the new year need to know that others are excited about it.

It's like Joseph settling in Nazareth. For some, living in this secluded Galilean town was just what they did. For Joseph and his family, it was a hiding place. Most neighbors never dreamed of leaving. Joseph and Mary knew that their son could never remain. As Matthew saw it, Nazareth was a way station, a linguistic link to 700-year-old messianic prophecies. Jesus and his neighbors were guaranteed to misunderstand each other.

A reader asks about that painful nexus of despair and hope, where a "broken heart" is slow to heal, yearnings and common sense collide, and violations of trust haven't yet motivated new behavior. How long will that nexus last?

Longer than you want, is one answer. Also, longer than the 104 minutes allotted to cinematic agony. But there is more to know.

If I am correct in believing that humanity is fundamentally interwoven, that we have been given to one another, and that love of neighbor is our highest calling, then the answer to "How long?" is this: As long as it takes for other people to notice your journey is different from theirs and for them to respond.

Our enemy isn't suffering, but the egocentrism and narcissism that prevent us from experiencing each other except as objects, threats, or gratification. If I cannot get outside myself, then I cannot see you as you are. If I cannot see you as you are, then I am blind to your differences, including the ways you are happy when I am sad, or broken when I am feeling whole.

A broken heart cries out, "See me!" The grieving feel invisible. The wounded feel isolated. The violated bristle with rage that no one else seems open to hearing. The abused feel imprisoned in a dirty secret. The oppressed are denied voice.

What Jesus did was to cut through this web of blindness, isolation, and secrecy. He spoke truth to those enmeshed in lies. He gave sight to the blind. He brought the wounded together. Talk to each other, he said. Listen to each other. Know each other. Love each other.

The most radical thing we Christians could do would be to connect the dots: to see our lives as bound together, to see the other as worthy, to share our journeys, to value our differences, to be curious about strangers, to give voice to the oppressed and sight to the blind, to know that someone nearby has a broken heart and nothing we do today will matter more than caring for that person.

QUESTION 74: "God, how do we love our neighbor, when so many things get in the way, such as spending too much time on issues that probably do not matter to you at all?"

John answered all of them by saying, "I baptize you with water; but one who is more powerful than I is coming; I am not worthy to untie the thong of his sandals." (Luke 3:16)

As a city boy, I grew up with street lights, car noises, sirens at all hours, and train whistles in the distance. Darkness was relative, not total. Silence meant more crickets and fewer trucks.

As an adult, I have lived mostly in suburbs, where street lights fight the darkness but also make it seem an enemy, and nighttime means fewer two-cycle engines and more heat pumps.

When we moved to this new house, we found ourselves in total darkness and silence. Four houses, quiet people, an unlighted country road. It made me nervous at first, but I quickly learned to treasure the subtle shadings of dawn, the floodlight of a full moon.

Then, two days ago, someone installed a street light. I suspect the neighbor to my left called the city because her teenagers waited in darkness for the school bus. Maybe it was the neighbor to my right, whose daughter comes home late from hospital duty.

Either way, the yellow light of a sodium-vapor lamp now floods our cul-de-sac, and tonight's full moon isn't as dramatic. My wife misses seeing the stars. I miss the peaceful envelope of darkened woods.

It doesn't matter. The city has found us, and that is that. It's like the acres of trees that were clear-cut last weekend for housing a mile away:

when they're gone, they're gone. I know that my eye will adjust to brighter lights. I know that a child's safety matters more than my delight in rural darkness.

Does it bother me? Yes. Am I going to stew about it? No. Some things are just part of life's unpredictability. Some things don't matter as much as others.

John the Baptist had perspective. He recognized his powers, but he knew Messiah was coming, with even greater powers. He had work to do, but within the context of the one who was coming. He stood aside, not because he had been defeated or deemed wrong, but because God's beloved was at hand.

Perspective has never been easy for Christians. We have tended to take an all-or-nothing attitude toward faith, as if the Christian enterprise were a delicate house of cards and any displacement would cause collapse. Doctrines extended to the smallest definitions. Moral codes left no behavior unregulated. Rather than embrace opposing ideas, we have fought and divided into hostile camps that insist their "truths" are absolute. We argue with vehemence to prevent the "domino effect" of one lapse unleashing a thousand lapses, one change causing a thousand changes, one acceptance of ambiguity undermining a thousand certainties.

If we are intellectually honest, we know that Jesus said hardly anything of what we insist is true, that we must torture the Old Testament to assemble scriptural weapons, and that religious history is a discouraging account of what happens when people lose perspective and become wedded to everything being equally true and equally important.

If we have lived at all, we know that it takes just one major tragedy for our certainties to be unmasked as absurd, our needs to be revealed as basic and our God as durable.

But staying in perspective is difficult when it is deemed a defeat or an error.

A reader asks how we can love our neighbor when so many small things get in our way. The answer is to follow the example of John the Baptist: to stand aside for the real messiah and to stop seeing God as fragile and the Christian enterprise as a house of cards.

QUESTION 75: "Will I ever be married with a family of my own one day?"

Simon answered, "Master, we have worked all night long but have caught nothing. Yet if you say so, I will let down the nets." When they

*had done this, they caught so many fish that their nets were begin-
ning to break.* (Luke 5:5–6)

Got a plane to catch. Hello, Kentucky! Want to talk basketball, Rick
vs. Coach K, Tubby vs. Roy, can anyone beat the ACC? Bring it on!

Oh, that isn't what this church leadership retreat is about? Hmm.
I wonder why not.

If Duke beat Carolina last night in overtime, if Louisville is on a tear
but Coach Pitino is sick, if UK is dropping from sight, and those subjects
are near to our hearts, why would we want to talk about the church
budget?

Okay, college basketball isn't your thing. Well, what is? To judge by the
"roadside questions" readers have been asking me, I'd say your questions
mainly concern faith, purpose, suffering, and relationships, in that order.

Church questions arise, too, but generally in reference to the pain
Christians cause one another in bickering. Not a single person has
mentioned the church budget, staff size, facilities, or the business affairs
of the church. Not a one. If anything, you have asked why church
leaders don't pay attention to what you really care about.

In a pew somewhere, a woman is asking, "Will I ever be married?" Is
she alone? Is everyone around her thinking about church staffing?
I doubt it. I'd say the questions tearing at their hearts and souls are like
hers. People bring to God questions about their lives and their world, not
questions about church.

Some might concern money, but their money, their job security, their
retirement-planning worries, their dread of growing old and entering
poverty.

Some might concern gut-wrenching decisions, but their decisions,
their wondering whether to stay married or try again, their vocations,
their inner conflicts between career and children, their quest for peace in
a noisy world.

Many concern faith, but their faith, not the church's official faith. No
one mentions apostolic succession, church doctrine, or conventions.
People wonder what happens after they die, how to know God is real,
how to obtain mercy.

Well, says the church leader, if we don't worry about budget, staff,
facilities, and other business affairs, who will? To which I respond, hire
an accountant, hire a human resources professional, hire a property
manager, or if money is tight, find someone in the pews who has those
skills.

The larger question is this: If you aren't hearing the questions your members actually are asking, who is? If you aren't listening and then leading the church forward in response to what you hear, what is the point of budget or staff?

Hmm. Maybe we should be talking basketball. Sounds safer.

Well, maybe we should be talking basketball. Or marriage, or politics, or job worries, or ailing family members, or the teenage son who is losing his way, or the daughter who is playing around. Not because those subjects are safer, but because it is what we truly care about. If anything, those subjects are more dangerous, more wrenching. If anything, we fuss about church in order to avoid life's direst dilemmas.

Enough of that! I say. Leaders must lead. They must climb the mountain that actually stands before them—which, believe me, isn't a mountain named "Annual Budget"—and look ahead to wilderness and promise. Then they must turn and look at the valley where people live. See the people, hear their cries, worry about them, and then join them with a call to move onward.

Or to use the image of Sunday's gospel, leaders must see their meager catch, feel their weariness, accept the reality that diligent effort in the wrong enterprise doesn't fill the nets, and then do it God's way.

QUESTION 76: "Jesus, when you take me to heaven, what will be my relationship with people I loved down here on earth, especially my husband who is with you now?"

Suddenly they saw two men, Moses and Elijah, talking to [Jesus]. They appeared in glory and were speaking of his departure, which he was about to accomplish at Jerusalem. (Luke 9:30–31)

A reader of my newspaper column takes me to task for failing to give a simple Yes-or-No answer to a question about same-sex marriage. He yearns for those "men of old who were filled with the Holy Spirit and under the direction of God were able to speak with definiteness and boldness."

If only life and faith were that simple. But I believe there was a reason Jesus himself avoided direct answers, especially Yes-or-No, but instead replied with parables of astonishing complexity and ambiguity, with words like "You say so," or not at all.

As I told this reader—a reply that probably won't satisfy him—"many questions are an opportunity to think for oneself, they are a window to larger understanding, and a simple Yes or No can cut off discernment, rather than advance it."

Some would turn the Bible into an answer book, as if all life questions and faith questions could be answered in the just-the-facts, encyclopedia-consulting method of answering.

But that is an abuse of Scripture, and it yields little food for the journey. Faith is about discovery, not facts, and it proceeds along a winding road marked by surprise encounters, unexpected companions, and learnings bought at great price. Jesus conferred sight, not information.

The first answer, therefore, to the reader's question about relationships in heaven is, we don't know for sure. No one has come back to tell us. Even Jesus, after his resurrection, spoke of how his disciples' lives would change on earth, not about what lay around the eternal bend.

But we do have glimpses. Take, for example, the transfiguration scene when Jesus stood with the long-deceased Moses and Elijah. Jesus was facing inevitable persecution at the hands of religious people. He was announcing dying time to his friends, so that they would be prepared, and he was on an internal journey of acceptance. I remember my mother doing the same.

Suddenly, God loved him in yet another new way. God sent companions to stand with him, perhaps to offer assurance, perhaps to give him unfettered, unfiltered room to speak. No need to record these words, and thereby give the religious something else to argue about. Just talk quietly about death. Peter, James, and John would have their own conversations about death later.

The disciples wanted more from this moment, maybe the yes-or-no certainties offered gladly by "men of old." But God wouldn't decipher or freeze the moment to make it acceptable to them.

What does this glimpse tell us? One lesson, of course, is to let God be God, to watch and to listen. Another is to trust that God's absolute commitment to love—a commitment that we taste, if only dimly, in our relationships on earth—occupies and defines the rest of life. God sees our wrestling with issues that matter—as well as our obsession with things that don't matter—and God has mercy and compassion. For there is so much that we don't yet know, and if we knew it, we would relax about life and stop shouting at each other.

And so God sends us glimpses—not encyclopedic answers, but glimpses—such as the dreams people report of seeing loved ones as they once were, smiling and welcoming, visions that aren't yet happening and cause us to ache, but speak of a tomorrow that is in God's hands and is trustworthy and good.

Chapter 9

Scripture

QUESTION 77: "Does God speak to people today, even after the Christian canon was closed? Does God speak differently to us in today's world than in the pre-canon world?"

The steward called the bridegroom and said to him, "Everyone serves the good wine first, and then the inferior wine after the guests have become drunk. But you have kept the good wine until now." (John 2:9–10)

Two friends are arguing.

Like many arguments, theirs combines cold logic, heated emotions, aggressive thrusts and defensive parries, overstated conclusions based on selectively remembered facts, more talking than listening, and wanting others to take sides.

The answer is to turn down the rhetoric, stop the accusations and blaming, move from haughty to humble, and look for compromise. But that can feel like losing.

I watch similar arguments tear apart the Christian movement. I am most troubled by battles within the Episcopal Church, because they hit home. But parallel arguments are splintering every denomination. These arguments consume extraordinary energy, waste financial and human capital, divert attention from actual human needs, cripple congregations, leave people feeling like orphans of a bitter divorce, and, in my opinion, thoroughly frustrate God.

We ought to be ashamed of ourselves. Instead, we think ourselves righteous, God's champions in holy battle. Our arrogance masquerades as piety, our power lust as truth seeking, our ignorance as knowledge.

Like our predecessors in a movement that historically has done more fighting than serving, we are willing to sacrifice anything to win.

We try to render God mute, small, and lifeless. In our quest for something called "biblical faith," we insist that God stopped speaking 2,000 years ago, and we turn even those beloved words into stones for throwing. We insist that God cares passionately about the topics that trouble us, no matter how small they are. We insist that God cannot be known except through our contested and stale words.

Meanwhile, the world turns, humanity suffers, children starve, the rich get richer, power flows, people fall in love, families form, death separates—and where is God? Where do we think God is? Waiting for our marching orders in the battle over some hot-button issue? I hope not. I hope that God is sitting with the wounded and arranging food for the hungry. I hope that God is warming hearts made cold by wealth and power. I hope that God is blessing our unions, holding our hands in grief, dreaming with us of better days. Otherwise, we fight over nothing.

A reader asks, "Does God speak to people today?" It is tragic that such a question even arises. Have we gotten so lost in our biblical studies, theologizing, and arguing over the authority of Scripture that we can do anything less than cry out, "Yes, God does speak, and I am hungry for those fresh words! I have tried to hoard yesterday's manna, but it grew stale, and I am starving."

Was it a tamed God who led the Hebrews across Sinai? No, it was a living God who heard their cries. Was it a frozen God who came to the Israelites in captivity? No, it was a passionate God who saw their fears. Was it a fastidious God who stood outside the tomb of Lazarus? No, it was one who wept at the cost of being messiah.

How could we possibly believe that this God went silent when a handful of bishops maneuvering for power declared the canon of the New Testament closed? Do we believe we have such control over God? Do we believe that God served the good wine long ago and nothing is left for us but stale dregs?

Some do, yes. The custodians of religion argue over authority, because they control the sacraments and pulpits, seminaries and rules, and from them they derive power. But the vast majority of us simply pray to a living God, because life is difficult and we need help.

QUESTION 78: "My Teacher, is their a new Word from the Lord"?

[Jesus] got into one of the boats, the one belonging to Simon,

and asked him to put out a little way from the shore. Then he sat down and taught the crowds from the boat. (Luke 5:3)

Our company continues to reinvent itself. Today we view a new organization structure, which assigns new duties, uses new words to describe our work, and draws new lines of relationship.

Will an org chart work magic? Not by itself. But over time, as people reenvision their roles and relate to one another in new ways, much will change, including the org chart itself. Those changes, in turn, can empower newness and growth to occur.

The one certainty is that, if we don't keep reinventing ourselves, we will surely go stale and weak, and eventually fail. The world around us is changing, our marketplace is changing, our business relationships are changing, and we who enter these doors for our livelihood are changing most of all. All those changes out there—babies being born, parents dying, houses being built, children leaving home, relationships changing—cause us to need new things from one another in here. Our company's structure, protocols, expectations, and dynamics must keep pace and remain flexible.

In my years in pulpit and pew, I have seen congregations edge up to reinvention and then pull away, generally in fear. Leadership groups try on new ideas. Individuals experience renewal events or life-transforming events. Pastor search committees see the body with new eyes. New clergy arrive.

The air stirs, ideas float freely, new people venture forward, new energy emerges, and many start a promising journey onward, usually in new relationships.

Then it stalls. People who found power or comfort in the old dispensation resist the new. They tell stories of how things used to be and remind everyone of their long tenure. Change becomes an issue, as if nonchange were somehow an option. People quote Scripture or church tradition to deny the validity of the new. Clergy come under fire, usually within eighteen months of starting a new pastorate. Lay leaders come under fire and drift away.

In our zeal for Scriptures that justify resistance to change, we fail to see that the Bible is about nothing but change. The ancients were "Hebrews," meaning "wanderers." The Christian enterprise is about movement, pilgrimage, venturing, dying to self, dying to old ways, hearing new words, entering new fellowships, tasting new wine, seeing God's new things.

A reader asks, "Is there a new word from the lord?" The answer is, Yes, there is nothing but new words. Look at what Jesus did with Simon. He went into the home of Simon's mother-in-law and healed her fever. He asked Simon to use his boat for a new purpose. He taught Simon to fish in a new way. He took Simon to new places, gave Simon a new name, sent him out on new work, changed his self-perceptions, changed his life, and gave him courage and wisdom he hadn't known before.

Can we possibly believe that such a call to newness died with Simon, or with the closing of the canon of the New Testament, or with the founding of our denomination or congregation, or the calling of the last pastor?

Not every new idea will succeed. Not every change is well-considered. Some reinvention will fail. Some might be dangerous. Some people will use change for mischief. But there is no denying change. If we don't reinvent ourselves, the world will reinvent us to suit its purposes. If we don't join hands and walk forward together, the power of darkness will isolate us, frighten us, turn us against each other, sap our energy, stir our bloodlust, cripple our venture, and land us, not in an unchanged world that feels safe, but in a darkened world where we are lost and alone.

Question 79: "How are we in this time and place to interpret Scripture?"

Then the devil took [Jesus] to Jerusalem, and placed him on the pinnacle of the temple, saying to him, "If you are the Son of God, throw yourself down from here, for it is written, 'He will command his angels concerning you, to protect you,' and, 'On their hands they will bear you up, so that you will not dash your foot against a stone.'"
(Luke 4:9–11)

My wife and I take seats in the balcony of our downtown armory, built in 1937 on the site of the City Market, used for National Guard training and later for dance festivals, biker shows, fencing competitions, and, tonight, the formal ball of Junior Cotillion.

Our tuxedo-clad son escorts a young lady onto the floor, and a final evening of instructional dancing begins. The evening's theme is international, so instead of their regular waltz, they do a "Swedish waltz." (Same steps, different name.) It isn't anything like the waltz I learned at age twelve.

To a lovely country song, they do a fox-trot. It has more sway than the version I learned. Better music, too. Their cha-cha (to a recording by Madonna, I think) has different steps, but the same invitation to let loose. The "electric slide" and "Cotillion stomp" are both new to me, but clearly a delight to the dancers.

There is a lot to interpret here. Were the dance versions I learned wrong or just different? How did the electric slide replace the tango? How did Nashville music get into ballroom dancing? Plus countless personal observations of my son coming of age.

Dancing and Scripture aren't the same—although the oldest Old Testament fragment tells of Miriam dancing as Pharaoh's troops drown—but consider the parallels.

It isn't enough to quote Scripture or to count the steps. Anyone can quote Scripture, even the devil, and can do so to justify virtually anything, from human slavery to slaughter of the Jews. Virtually every outburst of evil has had its Bible-thumping theologian. Dancing happens when you stop counting and learn to sway as two.

Nor is it enough to remember yesterday's dance with Scripture. Miriam's exuberant dance at death was a different time, different place. The Scripture-based certainties I learned as a child—such as white supremacy, Russia's evil, anti-Semitism—need to be reinterpreted. Exclusively male images of God seem too shallow. Our confrontations with actual evil require more than the sweetness of Sunday school pictures.

It's more than updating the old. Maybe my waltz was more accurate than my son's, maybe not. The point is learning to dance and to respect one's partner. My dancing class didn't teach line dancing—we learned "the Stroll" on our own—but that doesn't invalidate today's slide or stomp. I can judge the fashions on display, but to understand tonight's event, I need to see children as they are, not as how they compare with my youth.

It is helpful to know the history of where we came from. This armory hasn't always been here. It used to be a market, and before that probably had some role in the slave trading that supported nearby plantations, and before that some part of Native American life. What I see today isn't a permanent structure, but a product of cultural changes whose trajectory through time will tell me more about life than analyzing any one stop along the way. With Scripture, it is God's movement through time that matters more than the specific word God said at, say, the Red Sea crossing, or the cursing of Ahab, or the lamentation over Jerusalem.

Interpreting Scripture, therefore, is hard and humbling work. It means getting outside oneself—tonight is my son's night, not a reliving of my own adolescence—and seeing both life and God as they are now. That takes discernment, not memorization.

Chapter 10

Sexuality

QUESTION 80: "Do you think marriage can only be between a man and a woman?"

The scroll of the prophet Isaiah was given to [Jesus]. He unrolled the scroll and found the place where it was written: "The Spirit of the Lord is upon me, because he has anointed me to bring good news to the poor. He has sent me to proclaim release to the captives and recovery of sight to the blind." (Luke 4:17–18)

Well, there it is. The question that divides Christian denominations, the question that measures whether American Christians are in sync with Ugandans, the question that entered the American presidential campaign as a wedge issue, the question that could embroil the nation in a Constitutional amendment.

Or to be more accurate, there is the question that covers for other questions. Such as who gets to own church property, who gets public approval for their love, can we "clean up" modernity?

Or going deeper, there is the question that underlies all religious questions—can I believe one thing and you believe another and we both can be in right relationship with God?

In responding to this reader—a friend seeking guidance in her new role as grandmother—I need to say that this is a matter on which good and faithful people will disagree, often with a visceral energy that they assign to no other issue. Why such energy? Does the gut-wrenching signal something about God or about us?

I need to say, also, that we cannot look to church politicians, presidential campaigners, or TV evangelists for our answers. Their agendas are too complex and self-serving. We must wrestle with this question on our own. The best dialogue, it seems to me, would be, Here is what I think, now what do you think?

Here is how I answered my friend:

"My guess is that by the time this ugly election year is over, 'Christian marriage' will be so thoroughly politicized that we will be seeking another way to understand the ways people commit their lives to each other at a level of ultimate intimacy, fidelity, trust, and sacrifice.

"That way will have to do with the quality of their relationship, not their gender. Just as we moved beyond believing that Roman Catholics had to marry Roman Catholics, so we will move beyond a single view of Christian union.

"Will we call it 'marriage'? Probably not. Will it matter what we call it? Not really. People are already forming unions and families in diverse ways. Among the first people to open their hearts and homes to my dad after Mom died were a gay couple. That love means a whole lot more to me than gender issues.

"That's how I see it. How about you?"

Let's assume, now, that some agree with my answer and some think it wrong. What next? To my mind, that is the question we need to address. Not, how can I prove my case? But, how can we hold opposing views but still hold each other close? How can we love and serve God even as we disagree about what God is saying?

The tragedy isn't that we disagree, but that we dishonor each other and consider right opinion more important than servanthood.

When Jesus taught at the synagogue, he was handed a piece of tradition. He then chose how to use it. He didn't say that God had anointed messiah to dispense right opinion or rewards to the righteous. What he chose—and took as his mission—was Isaiah's call to "bring good news to the poor," "to proclaim release to the captives and recovery of sight to the blind."

That is a far cry from having right opinion about marriage or any other issue. That is servanthood, love in action, submission to the needs of others, an understanding of God as tenderhearted.

QUESTION 81: "What would Jesus say about same-sex marriages?"

[Jesus said,] "Blessed are you when people hate you, and when they exclude you, revile you, and defame you on account of the Son of Man. Rejoice in that day and leap for joy, for surely your reward is

great in heaven; for that is what their ancestors did to the prophets."
(Luke 6:22–23)

Over lunch at a restaurant that has apparently heard its customers
and hired a new chef, I finish *The E-Myth Revisited*, by Michael Gerber.

It is an airy but insightful essay on why small businesses fail. I suggest
it for church leaders, as well, for congregations also live or die, not by
facilities or friendliness, but by their leaders' entrepreneurial spirit,
commitment to consistency and service, and listening to customers.

Gerber says purchasing decisions are made irrationally and quickly,
and the wise entrepreneur will understand the customer's need for
emotional connection. Be listeners, not speakers. Focus on what the
customer needs, not on what you want to sell.

I immediately have two opportunities to apply these lessons. First is a
call to a business ally. Rather than ask why we did something, he tells us
we shouldn't have done it. Rather than explore an idea, he filters it
through his defensiveness. His needs are irrational—and we must
discern what they are.

I confer next with a colleague about a presentation to a prospective
client. Draft slides explain what we have to offer but don't build a bridge
to their situation. The slides are about us, not them.

A reader asks what Jesus would say about same-sex marriages. We
don't know for sure, of course, because Jesus said virtually nothing about
sex. It wasn't a concern to him. He taught about wealth, power, sacrifice,
and servanthood. But that isn't enough for us—or more likely, far too
much—so the Christian enterprise seems to turn now on issues of
sexuality.

What would Jesus say? I doubt that he would quote Leviticus. I doubt
that he would turn to the pope for advice or angry Anglicans or geneti-
cists or behavioral psychologists. He wouldn't see the U.S. Constitution
as a new Holiness Code.

I think he would call once again for that cloud which drives arguers
to their knees. He would say, "Listen to one another. Stop the bombast
and listen. Deep emotional needs are at work here. They won't be
resolved by adding up Scriptures, by marshalling cold logic or science, or
by hating, excluding, reviling, or defaming the other.

"No one gets 'victim points' for being the target of another's rage. The
point is to connect, not to stake out unassailable positions. Armies fight
over land, but Christians must form ever-widening circles."

I read a letter last week from a newly minted cleric to highly educated
parishioners, commanding them to stay within his doctrinal bounds. It

was astonishing in its arrogance. But I should be listening, not recoiling. Who is he? Why does he say such things? What emotions drive his words? How can I connect with his needs? For if I take him simply as the sum of his arguments, then I know too little.

The same goes the other way. If gay and lesbian couples are asking for civil and religious affirmation of their unions, we must be listening, not orating. Who are they? What needs drive them? What face of God do they represent?

These are persons—on both sides. Jesus had little use for the religious arguments of his day. I doubt he has any use for ours. Jesus sat with persons and loved them. He commanded his disciples to do the same.

Until we can turn the other cheek, so that our listening ear is closer to the other's heart, we are no better than those who persecuted Jesus for saying what they didn't want to hear and for loving those whom they hated.

Chapter 11

Change

QUESTION 82: "Where is God in the ordination process and which voices do we listen to?"

When [Jesus] had finished speaking, he said to Simon, "Put out into the deep water and let down your nets for a catch." Simon answered, "Master, we have worked all night long but have caught nothing. Yet if you say so, I will let down the nets." (Luke 5:4–5)

A friend and I discuss leadership. Our focus is business, but it could be any organization. Leadership is leadership.

Organizations, we agree, have a genius for exploiting the leader's weaknesses. As those who are led, we gossip about our leaders, use them as projection screens for our own issues, withhold information, impose absurd expectations, try to control them, and deny them empowerment.

We do so because we fear change, we fear loss of control, we resent not being in charge ourselves, or we don't want to work any harder, or because we have had too many negative experiences of bad leadership, from the "little Napoleon" to the incompetent desk jockey.

As leaders, in turn, we go through our own cycles of fear, addiction to control, resentments, manipulation, and a tendency to replicate self-destructive scenarios wherever we go.

Whether we are leader or follower, our leadership issues are about us, not about the setting or other persons. Self-examination, however, tends to be our last resort, so we lead poorly, follow poorly, and leave leadership vacuums in our wake, from the rudderless corporation to the poorly led committee to the functionally absent parent.

The sidelines of any venue—from businesses to churches to

families—are littered with wounded players begging not to be sent in again. The stands are filled with people wondering why the game is so lifeless. Where are the great presidents? Where are the powerful preachers? Why can't we face up to basic issues, from crumbling streets to crumbling congregations?

We sense the problem. How else could a local college justify charging $1,800 a head for a two-day leadership seminar by a little-known leadership guru? Would that a big check could buy a solution!

This, I believe, is the relevant context for leadership questions raised by numerous readers. They are wounded veterans of institutional warfare, religious and otherwise. Some are aspirants for ordination.

As I discovered when helping a denominational study of leadership conflicts, each story is unique and yet the same. You can listen to one beaten-up pastor and hear a thousand echoes. You could put leaders from any enterprise into a room, and they would tell the same stories of gossip, projection, and absurd expectations. Once they stopped blaming, you would hear the same overcompensation, control needs, fear of failure, pride, and unresolved anger. Followers see the falling numbers, weak finances, revolving-door memberships, and constant bickering, but what they don't see is their contributions to failure.

The reader asks a right question, but I would change its focus from ordination to leadership in general. A "call" to ministry is a call to acting out one's faith and baptism. Church employment is a different matter. It is a job, and what separates those who are adequate from those who are inadequate isn't the validity of "call," but the ability to lead. Congregations aren't dragged down by ordination practices, but by leaders and followers.

Consider Simon Peter. Simon became a capable leader, but he had to suffer first. He didn't know where to fish or how to fish. Simon resisted newness, wanted primacy, made stupid remarks, tried to freeze time, betrayed his master, and ran away in fear. At every stage, he required God's guidance and vanquishing. It wasn't keys or laid-on hands that enabled him to lead. It was working through his weaknesses, vainglory, obtuseness, pride, and fear.

When leaders are willing to endure that journey, they will have something to offer. When followers understand that is their journey, too, they will serve effectively. Until then, we are simply chasing jobs, privileges, and comforts.

QUESTION 83: "Where did Jesus experience unanticipated change in his life? How did it affect him in his ministry?"

*[Jesus] came down with [his disciples] and stood on a level place,
with a great crowd of his disciples and a great multitude of people
from all Judea, Jerusalem, and the coast of Tyre and Sidon. They had
come to hear him and to be healed of their diseases; and those who
were troubled with unclean spirits were cured. And all in the crowd
were trying to touch him, for power came out from him and healed
all of them. (Luke 6:17–19)*

Saturday evening is a mellow time at the Louisville and Cincinnati
airports.

Coming home from leading a church retreat, I feel a swirl of
emotions. Self-doubt, for I took a new tack in this retreat and wonder
whether it worked. Gratitude, from having been welcomed by a remark-
able group of people. Pleasure, from small surprises like seeing Louisville
for the first time.

I feel pensiveness about my life's fragile balance of marriage, family,
job, house, freedom, faith, and health.

If we could step back from our conflicts, the relentless coarsening of
our culture, the corrosion of our corporate and governmental ethics,
and our headlong dash into self-destructive wars and waste, I think we
would see lonely travelers worrying about tomorrow.

Many search for some rock to stand on. In response, hypocritical and
self-serving rock providers swoop in, like drug dealers invading a school
yard.

They fix blame, name enemies, and encourage scapegoating. They
offer simple solutions to complex issues. They encourage denial of
reality and escape into nostalgia. They divide crowds into Us and Them.
They choose leaders who stoke rage and fear. They seize control of basic
institutions.

They paint ugly pictures—a nation welcoming only people like them,
a culture needing to be cleansed of the not-Us, a faith grounded in rules
and revenge—all the while claiming to be the true advocates of home
and holy.

Meanwhile, lonely travelers are left with their questions and doubts.

Who are these providers of phony rocks? They aren't necessarily
conservatives or liberals, fundamentalists or freethinkers. They are those
who speak in absolute certainty, who turn life's normal angst into scapegoating, who hijack God as their champion, who assert that some lives
matter more than others, some deserve not to be free, some are so wrong
that their voices must be stilled.

In their deceit, they give a bad name to true fundamentalism, which was focused on personal salvation, congregational polity, devotion to Scripture, and self-sacrificial mission work, before ideologues seized power and began to institute a rigid monolithic structure. They give a bad name to liberalism—true liberalism grounded in free thought and free expression. They make Jesus seem elitist and the Bible a cache of weapons.

A reader asks if Jesus ever experienced change. Yes, the teaching of Jesus changed dramatically. He went from teaching in synagogues to teaching on hillsides. He went from confirming tradition to contradicting tradition. He went from expecting acceptance to expecting rejection. He went from redeemer messiah to "suffering servant" to apocalyptic "Son of Man" to silent victim. His healings changed, his relationships with the disciples changed, and to the extent that we can discern his internal journey, his emotions and self-awareness changed.

What caused Jesus to change? Events like standing on the plain amid lonely and worried travelers and feeling their pain. Jesus interacted with humanity, and those interactions touched him so deeply that he allowed himself to change direction, to step beyond tradition, to hear new voices, and to understand both himself and God in new ways.

The glory of Jesus isn't that he had it all figured out when he started, but that he learned along the way. He learned by loving. And that is what I find most frightening about today's religious ideologues. They dread real learning, gained through discovery, dialogue, and discernment, so they don't dare teach love, for love transforms. They can only teach hate.

QUESTION 84: "What does it mean to be 'made in your image'?"

[Jesus] went down to Capernaum, a city in Galilee, and was teaching them on the sabbath. They were astounded at his teaching, because he spoke with authority. (Luke 4:31–32)

Five years ago today, I joined two men in founding a company.

At first, my roles were improbably broad: technician, consultant, trainer, documenter, entrepreneur, planner, executive, salesperson, programmer, travel coordinator, coffee maker. The three of us had to do it all.

As our company grew, I yielded most roles to others, and my work became focused as consultant and director of strategic initiatives. That focus hasn't been easy or painless. It was fun traveling the world as a jack-of-most-trades. Some days I look at others doing work that I did just six months ago, and I feel adrift.

In order to serve our clients, however, we must deepen our skills, broaden our capabilities, and standardize our performance. To do that, the founders must make room for the skills, personalities, and needs of others. We must allow our company's image to change from three guys to a diverse multitude, with a corporate personality larger and more complex than any one of us.

For some time now, church folk have worked on one end of this process. We have understood that a healthy Christian community requires many gifts, many ministers, many access points, many voices. This has been both liberating and frustrating. It requires clergy to let go and to share significant work with others. It requires lay leaders to stop treating clergy as if they should be omnicompetent. It requires lay members to stop being spectators and consumers and to become ministers. It requires paid staff to behave more professionally. It shifts the focus from hiring and budgeting to serving persons, which means assessing their needs, measuring our responses, holding ourselves accountable for being effective, not just well-intentioned.

This has been a wrenching process and the cause of substantial conflict. But even harder work lies ahead.

This process has another end. That is where we understand God as having a richly diverse and complex nature, and we are forced to recognize that no one person, no one truth, no one assertion or inherited value says it all. We tend, you see, to project our own image onto God. Letting go of projection will be far more difficult than sharing the duties and privileges of ministry.

It is one thing to let women serve at the altar, but quite another to see God as having a feminine nature. It is one thing to countenance gay clergy and members, but quite another to see them as reflecting a fundamental aspect of God's being. We integrate our pews, but do we yet welcome a multiracial God? We pray alongside Muslims, but can we understand Islam as possessing a legitimate portion of God's truth? We are okay with letting children come close, but what about lepers, outcasts, criminals, people so unlike us that we are offended by the idea that they, too, reflect the image of God?

This work will shake our foundations, because it means God is far larger than anything we have countenanced, and therefore is beyond our desire to limit and to define. We will be forced to see that much of God resides outside Scripture, outside our tradition.

We must imagine more than we will ever see, and become humble in the face of what we cannot control. We must listen to all of Jesus—not just the few phrases and actions that get us through the day, but his full and distressing "authority." Then we must listen to all of creation for what it says of the author. Jesus told us there would be more. Now we must listen for the more.

"What does it mean to be 'made in your image'?" It means far more than we ever thought possible.

QUESTION 85: "Why are people so afraid of the idea that God believes we are all equally special and deserving of grace?"

[John said,] "And all flesh shall see the salvation of God." (Luke 3:6)

Frustrated with congestion on my weekday drives, I feel a need for the open road. My son joins me for a back-roads outing.

"Open road" means skipping the interstate, an 80-MPH version of what I endure every day. We head west on a state highway, through tobacco and textile towns whose moment has passed.

The road is open, curvy, and hilly enough to require downshifting and cornering, rather than aiming and avoiding. Feeling alone on the road is great.

We cruise into a one-time tobacco town and stop at Pete's Burgers. We are the only unknown faces, so people stare. It is an oddly affirming contrast to urban anonymity, where no one stares or cares.

We drive on to a city where we once lived. At my son's request, we drive past his favorite park and out to a house that has mixed memories for me but remains golden for him. We take familiar streets to an ice cream shop and on to a bookstore. Familiar places, but not that first familiar face. I am surprised. How could six years here not have tamed the anonymity?

Religion seems to answer questions of the moment. Yes, it also addresses eternal quandaries like death, and whatever question it addresses, religion dons the mantle of eternal wisdom and truth. But if you stand back, you see the momentary.

Early Christianity searched for identity in a world already populated by Judaism, Greek philosophy, Roman imperialism, and Eastern mysticism.

Later, Christianity responded to superstition and fear in a darkening world, made common cause with monarchs in a mad quest for gold, fought enlightenment when knowledge and freedom threatened its franchise, and became house theologian for slavery and genocide.

Christians did a lot else, of course. They preserved knowledge, founded universities and hospitals, gave a measure of hope and dignity to the oppressed, married and buried the faithful, encouraged civility, promoted artistic beauty, and employed Bach.

But the dark side was always present, shaping the Christian movement's self-understanding and fostering excesses like the Crusades, the Spanish Inquisition, and the Puritans' bland singing of Psalm 2 as they massacred the Pequots.

Now that Christianity has become a worldwide phenomenon embraced increasingly by people of color, it becomes impossible to think of a single "movement" proclaiming a single message. Identity questions are back at the fore, especially in regions like Africa and India, where Christianity collides with energetic Islam; and in regions like Europe and America, where "none" is the fastest growing religious preference.

In America the underlying trauma is anonymity. More and more, people feel cut off from community, safe only indoors, treated as dispensable employees and gullible shoppers. For a time, neighborhood churches eased our angst as we moved from farm to city, from small town to suburb. But urban sprawl continued and anonymity worsened.

Today, Christianity's emerging face is the religious equivalent of Wal-Mart: megachurches located on highways, reached by automobile, offering one-stop shopping, devoted to pleasing customers and promoting name brands as a substitute for identity.

Gone are the nuances and ambiguities that come from walking the streets and encountering people's unique lives. Gone are the compromises that enable marriages to endure, neighbors to get along, and towns to survive changing fortunes. Gone is any delight in diversity, discovery, and doubt.

The winning strategy now is triumphalism: we are right and everyone else wrong, we alone have God's approval, we alone are worthy, we alone know truth. Everyone else is lesser, indeed expendable. To compete, smaller congregations embrace the same intolerant tribalism.

Now there is no room for accepting the other as simply different. They must be portrayed as dangerous. They must be stopped.

── ⌒ **Chapter 12** ⌒ ──

Job

QUESTION 86: "Lord, what shall I do?"

[Jesus said,] "When the season came, [the owner] sent a slave to the tenants in order that they might give him his share of the produce of the vineyard; but the tenants beat him and sent him away empty-handed." (Luke 20:10)

My conviction—that seeing the small stages of our journeys gives us confidence for tackling the large—now comes to a test.

On Monday, after five years of helping to grow our consulting firm from three partners to twenty-one employees, I learned that our growth had far outpaced our contracts and that a major restructuring of the firm was required. My job as senior consultant and director of strategic initiatives was among those being eliminated.

No rancor, no questions about my competence or performance, just financial numbers that weren't making sense. I have known about the gloomy finances and am not surprised by the outcome.

Now what? After hearing the news, I went for a walk with another former employee, a man of deep faith. He reminded me, as today's reader knows, that the question of what next starts with knowing whom to ask. I don't believe that God has a plan all worked out, but I do believe that God has a desire for my life, and that any plans I make must not send that desire away "empty-handed."

First, I know not to panic and not to drown in self-doubt. I have changed careers before. As Gloria Gaynor sang in her anthem of determination and hope, "I've got all my life to live, I've got all my love to give and I'll survive, I will survive."

Second, I know I am not alone. I have an amazing family, grounded in faith and tempered by shared struggles. I am surrounded by a great cloud of witness, including you who read these words. I have a loving God as my constant companion.

Third, I have a dream. The dream has been building for years—it launched these meditations—and has been taking specific shape over the past several months. It is to take the "land" that God has given me—skills like writing and teaching, a quick and creative mind, an ability to think outside the box—and to work more intentionally in that vineyard.

A reader asks—millions of people ask—"Lord, what shall I do?" That is never an idle question, and at times it becomes the question above all others. We have but the one life to live, and how we pour out that life is among our most solemn concerns. Entire industries are built on making that a trivial concern, a consumer whim, or someone else's choices. But they lie. None of us has an infinite array of options, but we do choose whether or not to love, to serve, to trust, to ask for God's help, and to press onward. Life's significant choices, in other words, remain ours to make.

We are tenants on someone else's land. Some tenants grow one crop, some grow another. Some tenants produce in abundance, some have modest output. Some tenants live well, some live meagerly. But we are all tenants, given "land" by another and given time to make our way. The delusion that will kill us is to think ourselves the owners.

What any of us does next must start in knowing whose life we are farming. That knowledge conveys obligation—the owner's share—but it also grounds us in God's authority. That authority, in turn, has never been about power and control, for we aren't slaves. God's authority is about love, compassion, mercy, and hope.

Whatever happens next, that is ground I can walk and farm with confidence.

QUESTION 87: "Are there some sins that can't be forgiven?"

[Jesus said,] "So [the tenants] threw [the son] out of the vineyard and killed him. What then will the owner of the vineyard do to them? He will come and destroy those tenants and give the vineyard to others." (Luke 20:15–16)

As I chart a career course, this is a time of many decisions for me. Some are large, some are small, and some will seem trivial but prove to be momentous. In all of them, I know my potential to decide poorly.

I have made poor decisions before, often after considerable planning, even after prayer. No amount of wisdom or faith prevents error.

I don't recall too many instances of making a decision knowing that it was a wrong decision. Wrongness tends to be a surprise.

The question is how to deal with error, failure, bad judgment, and decisions that seem aboveboard at the time but prove to have a seamy underside. For all will occur. I believe that God is lavish in forgiveness, for God knows us well. But, as a reader asks, are there some wrong decisions that are beyond forgiveness?

The world of religion is rife with assured answers to that question. Some believers can speak with astonishing certainty about those actions so offensive to God that eternal damnation ensues. Their certainty tends to follow a certain doctrinal preference and to draw selectively from the Scripture. We disagree, therefore, on what God finds excessive. Even the Ten Commandments, in our minds at least, have exceptions.

Rather than getting cagey with God and trying to outguess the score-keeper, maybe we should be asking the question differently. The point of sin isn't eternal consequence, but destruction today. God's forgiveness probably is more lavish than we can accept. But so is God's determination that we be free—including freedom to suffer consequences of our actions.

In the parable of the vineyard, for example, the tenants committed a worse crime than any of us might consider: killing the owner's son in order to claim his inheritance. As a consequence, the owner destroyed the tenants and gave the vineyard to others.

To the early church, that parable explained the quandary of Israel: chosen by God as a holy people but then rejected when they turned against messiah. It also reinforced the belief that sin leads to eternal death.

But the parable made no mention of eternity. It said that killing the son led to destruction and loss of the land. But later, in his sacrifice on Calvary, Jesus looked at the same sinners and said, "Father, forgive them; for they do not know what they are doing."

Shortly after that, the light over Jerusalem failed and the curtain of the temple was torn in two. In 70 A.D., the temple itself was destroyed. Destruction did happen. But so, if the passion and resurrection are to be believed, did the promise of forgiveness.

In other words, we are responsible for this life, but not for eternity. Our actions have consequences now, but God takes charge later. The tenants lost land and life, but not an eternity grounded in forgiveness.

To some believers, that isn't a pleasing concept. Their faith is grounded in a straight-up trade: eternal life in exchange for good behavior. But if we know ourselves, we know that error, failure, stupidity, and hubris are always within easy reach. Good behavior seems more elusive.

The wages of such sin are indeed death: death to love, death to relationships, death to emotional well-being, death to self-regard. God doesn't protect us against such dying. But there comes a point, as on Calvary, where God's mercy and forgiveness take over.

If we are open to repentance, that mercy and forgiveness can be ours now, and the next days in this life can be brighter. If not, we depend on God to save us later.

QUESTION 88: "When do you stay, and when do you go? From relationships to problems to ideas that may not be working. It seems like walking away is sometimes the best option, and sometimes tenacity prevails. I wonder what wisdom Jesus would give."

[Jesus] looked at [the people] and said, "What then does this text mean: 'The stone that the builders rejected has become the cornerstone'? Everyone who falls on that stone will be broken to pieces; and it will crush anyone on whom it falls." (Luke 20:17–18)

From previous career changes I have learned five lessons. I think these lessons apply to other changes, from launching a family to ending a relationship to making a sale to entering a retirement center:

First, don't waste time. Every minute counts. I have a certain period to establish a new course. Honoring time doesn't mean working every hour of the day, for time with family and friends is precious, too. But time wasters such as telemarketers, junk mail, pointless arguments, and empty gatherings must go.

Second, stick to reality. Cash, for example. Easy credit is a thief, and banks that prey on our neediness deserve to be acquired and to suffer the indignities of "restructuring." Better to do without than to assume the shackles of debt. Avoid anything that feeds denial of the current situation as requiring new behaviors.

Third, accept help. For the most part, people are good. Some have more capacity for giving than others, and some have more help to give. But people do want to help. The obstacle to helpfulness usually isn't the other; it's oneself and one's pride.

Fourth, change course. The future will be different. Resistance to change is a conceit of the lazy and fearful. We spend way too much time being nice about change. Those who fight change are serving only themselves and, by denying someone else's freedom to breathe and to grow, are abusive.

Fifth, trust in God. God has a big and loving heart, and God cares about us. God's caring will take many forms, some of them predictable, most of them surprising. Trusting in God means letting go of control, and saying Yes to life.

These aren't lessons directly enumerated in the gospel, but I think they are what Jesus was saying.

His message to the people was, first, the time is now, the kingdom of God is at hand, be alert, don't waste time.

Second, know yourself as you are, not as you imagine yourself to be. See the truth about wealth and privilege; see your would-be leaders for what they are, study the seasons.

Third, love one another, which means receiving love as well as giving it. Don't lose your identity in fear or hubris.

Fourth, allow God to do new creation. Everything is being made new, including much that you hold dear. Without change, there will be no future. Change isn't an option. Those who resist change for themselves are delusional, and those who resist change for others are serving only themselves and need to be ignored.

Fifth, look around, look for manna on the ground, hear the demoniacs and lepers who know truth, see calm in the storm, allow God to be God.

A reader asks when to stay and when to go. The answer is contextual, of course, and loaded with subtleties. But I'd say the lessons apply. If a stone is being rejected, that rejection must be taken seriously (given time), experienced (taken as reality), put alongside true value (self-worth, true friends), trusted as the future's cornerstone, and discussed with God. Staying or going must be grounded in reality, not denial, nostalgia, inertia, or stubbornness.

Onward doesn't necessarily mean out the door, but onward is reality, and onward with God is ultimate reality. For we were born to be free, not slaves; citizens of God's kingdom, not fearful inhabitants of someone else's tidy preserve; lovers and the loved, not integers in someone else's calculation.

QUESTION 89: Pray that I may discern God's will in this part of my life.

Then [Jesus and his disciples] went on to another village. (Luke 9:56)

A friend is considering a new job. Tough decision: loss and gain, grief and exhilaration, risk and possibility.

I know the feelings. I have had four distinct careers, and within each career several new assignments, and within each assignment new duties. Here is what I have learned:

First, no job is perfect. Work is aptly named. All jobs have their measure of tedium, unrewarding colleagues, and stupid politics.

Second, no job-decision process is perfect. Any change involves risk. We never see enough, ask all the right questions, or attain unemotional objectivity. How else does Detroit sell cars? Refusal to decide is no better. Different risks, is all.

Third, no job change will resolve personal issues. We carry ourselves with us from job to job. The way to make our lives better is to make better decisions about life, not work.

Fourth, a job isn't a marriage. Any employer who demands the prerogatives of marriage—from total fidelity to intimacy—is demonic. A job is a job, not a union of lives into something larger and more perfect. That is true of church jobs, as well as secular, by the way.

Fifth, pay matters. Feeling underpaid saps the spirit. Feeling fairly compensated builds self-respect.

Sixth, pay isn't the answer. Feeling valued matters more. So does feeling competent.

Seventh, getting a job isn't the same as getting a life. But not having a job while wanting one can break one's heart.

Eighth, change is good. Risk is good. Trying new things is good. Challenging oneself is good. Changing careers is good. Not always possible, of course, but when possible, worth considering for the sheer adventure of it.

Finally, we can learn from Jesus. A certain piety wants to paint him as unchanging, consistent from cradle to grave. In fact, he changed constantly. He changed duties. He went from place to place. He kept reconstituting the circle around him. His self-understanding evolved. He placed no apparent value on being consistent. He apparently saw the religious establishment's quest for time-tested, unchanging truths as absurd, a denial of God, a pious tool for clinging to control. Looking backward, as he saw it, was no way to plow a field.

Jesus seemed to take work as a given. He said little about it. He was more concerned about how people handled wealth and treated one another.

How does my friend decide about changing jobs? With his eyes open, for starters. He needs to examine his motivations for thinking about a new job and an employer's motivations for wanting him. Do they want him as he is and can be, or have they fabricated some artificial image that they want him to fill?

Looking forward, not backward. Years past are gone. He cannot reclaim them or rewrite them. The question is, What next?

With an eye to personal safety. All employers are a little crazy—they're just folks, after all—but some are sick, dysfunctional, destructive. A congregation that beat up its last pastor is likely to beat its next. A "little Napoleon" who sowed dissent and tension yesterday isn't likely to discover effective management tomorrow. Control issues don't disappear. Neither does bullying, micromanaging, or exploitation. (The same is true of employees, of course.)

With an eye to possibility. The most interesting thing about tomorrow is what it might be. Things don't always get better. But upward or downward, tomorrow is the venue of possibility, and that is inherently fascinating. Or ought to be. If the new job doesn't seem any different, what's the point?

And, as always, with an eye to what really matters. Our partners and children probably care less about our jobs than we do. Our bodies might be happier if we ratcheted down the stress. Our golf games surely would improve. So it's a matter of balance. Will the new job improve one's balance?

— ୬ Chapter 13 ୬ —

Words before the Cross

QUESTION 90: "How do I discern your voice?"

[Jesus said,] "Father, if you are willing, remove this cup from me; yet, not my will but yours be done." (Luke 22:42)

A woman stumbles as she enters Sunday school class. Our teacher immediately stands to offer his arm. The room stirs with concern.

In worship, a tenor stands to sing a solo. He admits to strong emotions and begs forgiveness if he cannot finish. He does finish. His passion is stunning.

So is the passion of today's preacher. It isn't the smooth soaring of a practiced emotionalist, but a gawky rending of the fabric, bearing the message: I care so deeply about hunger that I risk speaking awkwardly.

Such passion reaches into the pews, not as blood-soaked entertainment, but as an invitation to care. Cinematic values are absent. No one will mistake teacher, tenor, or preacher for anything other than believers doing their best. But their invitation to care cuts deeply. For its focus isn't what happened to Jesus in a vivid but safe retelling of ancient events. Its focus is today: a woman needing help, friends hungry for hope, strangers hungry for food. It is an invitation not to watch, but to stand and care.

I am tired of jousting with people who have seen the movie *The Passion of the Christ* and think they have seen it all. The proof of that pudding will be whether they lead different lives. I don't believe faith is that simple—watch a movie, get right with God. But if 126 minutes of cinema violence can change their lives for the better, so be it.

Instead, I want to reflect on "Six Words before the Cross," the words

Jesus spoke before his trial and torture, words that explain why and what and reach disturbingly into our lives.

First word: "Father, if you are willing, remove this cup from me; yet, not my will but yours be done."

A reader asks how to discern God's voice. That is what it sounds like. It is the voice of one who, after months of ministry, figures out where it is leading and submits humbly. It is the voice of one striving steadfastly to touch humankind with grace, being misunderstood and exploited, having the worst evils done in his name, but still willing to care.

It is the voice of patience when all others would lose patience. It is the voice of forgiveness when all others would seek revenge. It is the voice of justice when all others would seek advantage. It is the voice of passion when all others would stand by watching.

It is a lonely voice, like the voice of a tenor who says, I am going to stand here all alone and sing my faith. It is the voice of a mother who sits, unobserved, uncelebrated, with a needy child and sings softly of peace. It is the voice of a father who sees his child across the way and rushes to embrace him. It is the voice of a child who relaxes into the arms of love and then rises to stand and care.

It isn't the voice of heroism, as the world knows heroism. It is a voice of submission, a losing of self in order for another to find self, a losing of life in order for another to live. It is the voice of letting go, not control. It is the voice of daring to be awkward, not orderly and tidy. It is the voice that sees the moment, not the precedent, and stands to help.

It is this voice that the world seeks to stop. For it is this voice that gives the lie to humanity's pride and vainglory, humanity's determination to exert control, humanity's fear of truly being known, humanity's fear of being loved without measure.

Jesus' first drops of blood were shed in Gethsemane, when he said Yes to God: "not my will but yours be done."

QUESTION 91: "Now that I have accepted my divorce, forgiven my ex for what happened, forgiven myself for not seeing it coming, and adjusted to the role of single male, will love ever come my way again, even if I am scared of being hurt that much again?"

[Jesus] said . . . "Why are you sleeping? Get up and pray that you may not come into the time of trial." (Luke 22:46)

A loved one asks my advice on a career decision.

My first reaction is to be protective. One course sounds dangerous—physically hazardous, professionally off-track—while another course sounds safe and logical, more likely to pay off financially.

But then I do more exploring and thinking, and recognize the distinction between growing a career and growing as a person.

"As you can plainly see from my own experience," I tell him, "careers come and go. But who you are as a person travels with you and shapes your relationships, your marriage and family, your citizenship, your life skills, your faith, and your sense of well-being. The issue, as it comes more into focus for me, isn't what next step will lead to an ideal career path, but what will help you grow as a person."

We have a choice, in gospel terms, between "sleeping" and "trial." To be awake, alive, alert, engaged in life, and true to our humanity, there is no avoiding trial. Suffering happens. Whether you are raising a child or attempting romance, moving beyond the past or imagining the future, it hurts. Not all the time, but more of the time than our culture, with its deification of comfort and safety, thinks necessary.

There are no safe jobs, safe careers, safe choices. As millions can testify, virtually all employment is temporary. And while no one sets out to have multiple marriages, transitory friendships, numerous houses, and episodic interests, most of life is temporary, as well.

We might not be pioneers crossing the prairie, but neither are we settlers laying foundations that will last forever. We are pilgrims, waking up each morning on ground that we might be leaving soon, moving toward promises, leaving vistas that once seemed appealing, weary of constant change and yet unable to stop change.

We can try to stay asleep and avoid the day's trial. That's what Jesus saw his disciples trying to do. While he struggled in Gethsemane with a sudden awareness of where his messianic ministry was leading, they were sleeping. If this is the best they could do, they should pray not to "come into the time of trial."

But they could do better, as they showed later, when they faced their own Gethsemanes and chose to serve God. So can we all. That is an amazing fact about humankind: our durability. We can't avoid trial, self-inflicted or other-inflicted, but we can survive it, and we can grow through suffering.

A reader asks if love will ever come his way again. My answer is Yes, as long as he stays awake and is willing to be hurt again. If he needs assurances, comfort, and safety, then probably not.

We live in a culture where pain is considered a mistake, suffering avoidable, self-sacrifice foolish, risk "manageable," and faith passive, a righteous form of entertainment, where all the heavy lifting has already been done.

Imagine our surprise, then, when things don't work out, when a marriage fails, when a job evaporates, when a carefully managed career plan comes up empty, when even success leaves us hungry, when nothing seems certain.

In the consulting business this is called "expectation management." Our challenge, it seems to me, is to get our expectations in line with reality. Risk is unavoidable. So is pain. So is error. So is frustration. Instead of looking for ways to factor out the trials of life, we should prepare ourselves to grow through them, by trusting God enough to stay awake when trial looms.

QUESTION 92: "How to walk and talk to glorify the Trinity in the midst of civilization's challenges? Crisis? Collapse?"

Jesus said . . . "Judas, is it with a kiss that you are betraying the Son of Man?" (Luke 22:48)

ANN ARBOR, MICHIGAN—This seems a strange place to be thinking of civilization's collapse. Prosperous university town, proud home to the nation's largest college football stadium, major research center, handsome even in pre-spring.

But a longtime resident tells about a man who won big on the state lottery, immediately spent big, and is rapidly blowing the rest at Detroit's new gambling casinos.

"Michigan has legalized gambling?" I ask. How desperate is this state?

Yes, she says, a former mayor led the charge, and now Detroit has three casinos. There, she says, people are gambling away their paychecks, credit card balances, and savings. Parents have left children in cars for eight-hour stretches in freezing temperatures. "Gambling is a far worse addiction than crack or alcohol," she says.

The casinos are seductive, says a nongambler, who went once with a friend. No windows, no clocks, no mirrors ("They don't want people seeing themselves"), just bright lights, pounding music, and the lure of easy money just one slot-machine pull away.

Meanwhile, community agencies struggle to provide educational enrichment to children, while their parents struggle to make a living, as well as to provide food to the homeless and diverse forms of assistance to others.

Leaving aside the usual pieties about people making their own beds, what you have are islands of prosperity, swamps of abuse and neglect, and large, persuasive industries devoted to exploiting the weak and desperate. What happens when a state preys on its own people? What happens when the smart and fortunate find safe places to live and drive elsewhere with doors locked?

Where is the outrage? Where are the churches? Maybe they fought casino gambling and lost. If so, why? How did their influence get so small? Maybe the labor unions put up a fight, too. What happened to their influence? What about the other supposedly civilizing institutions, like the University of Michigan? Did their voice also count for nothing? Or were any of these voices even raised in resistance?

Who has voice for decency? The religious right wing prattles on about moral decay, by which they inevitably mean sexual ethics with which they disagree. If our civilization collapses, however, it won't be over sex. It will be over exactly the situation being lived out here: government preying on its citizens, widening gaps between rich and poor, the fortunate hoping to buy safety while the desperate multiply, and the historic voices for goodness choosing silence.

Thus happens betrayal. Jesus was betrayed by one of his own, perhaps the very disciple in whom he placed greatest trust. In his final hours, Jesus was abandoned by all others, except a few brave souls who watched from afar.

A reader asks how to "walk and talk" in a faithful manner as civilization struggles. The answer is this: noisily. No more silence. No more safe havens for the pious. No more quiet churches bickering politely about the past. No more feeding the insatiable beast of self-serving fundamentalism. No more colorful banners, cheery music, and sexuality debates while other people suffer.

This is a time for noisy footsteps, for standing up to forces of darkness, for shouts of outrage over what our culture is doing to its people. No more fascination with a fabricated "passion," while real tragedy happens down the street. No more pretending that our fortunes aren't all bound together. No more kisses of betrayal. No more silence.

QUESTION 93: "What one focus—personal as well as worldwide—would help most to lead us to a peaceful coexistence with all those who are 'different' from us?"

Jesus said, "No more of this!" And he touched his ear and healed him. (Luke 22:51)

Families gather in darkness outside our children's downtown school. This magnet school draws students from all over. Families are strangers to one another. We remain beside our cars.

Five tour buses pull into view. Parents move to the drop-off point, gather their children, and scatter.

On our drive home, my son tells me about the medieval battle scene that was their destination. He talks about maces, pikes, lances, broadswords, and shields, and how staff were trained to use them realistically. They sat at long tables decorated with certain colors and were instructed to cheer for knights wearing those colors.

I don't grasp why they traveled four hours to watch knights fight. Maybe it culminated a section on European history, a story that would be difficult to tell without scenes of violence.

Perhaps tomorrow, after he has slept off the excitement, I will explain how those medieval knights served two masters, church and crown, the twin pillars of the so-called "medieval synthesis." Each sought to advance its cause by alternately cooperating with, manipulating, and resisting the other. That cause was power, the ability to coerce people and through coercion to govern and to profit.

The crown's aims are no mystery. The lust for mastery and wealth always beats strong in the human breast. But the church's side is perplexing. As we see in our day, religion is guided by more than power lust. If it were just power, wars would be shorter.

Religion wants more. Religion wants the satisfaction of being right. Religion looks at a parking lot filled with strangers and tends to divide them into good and bad, sheep and goats, those being saved and those not, worthy and unworthy.

Religion names sides and, to the extent that it has any leverage, encourages or requires adherents to pick a side and to fight. Weapons vary from social snobbery to bombs, but the impulse is the same: we are right, all others are wrong, and our rightness requires us to win by any means.

Religion usually explains its warfare as a service to God, a holy crusade without which God would be lost. It isn't just that God prefers us, but that God needs us to win, and any behavior that doesn't serve the cause of victory is offensive to God. Our eternity and God's eternity are both at stake. There is no room for compromise, nuance, or doubt. Negotiation and power sharing are anathema.

A reader asks what "one focus" would facilitate peace. I doubt there is a simple formula. But I do think religion needs to examine its determination to be right.

Rightness gets us off message. It diverts our attention from servanthood to victory, from seeing needs to seeing opposition, from invitation to invective, from humility to hubris, from open doors to closed ranks, from exploration to exclusion. In our search for right opinion, we become smaller, less noble.

Clinging to rightness makes us easily manipulated. As modern politicians discover to their delight, throwing a few favors to religion will win access to member lists and preaching content. If we can be lured into marginal issues like sexuality, we won't have the cohesion or focus to notice the truly deplorable and destructive. We will wear ourselves out on trivialities and have nothing left for meddling in humanity's actual travail.

We need to hear the command that Jesus gave to his disciples when they drew swords to protect him. "No more of this!" he said. The Son of God doesn't require us to take up arms. Jesus doesn't enlist us in a battle for power or right opinion. Jesus asks us to serve, as he served.

QUESTION 94: "Why do bad things happen?"

Jesus said to the chief priests, the officers of the temple police, and the elders who had come for him, "Have you come out with swords and clubs as if I were a bandit? When I was with you day after day in the temple, you did not lay hands on me. But this is your hour, and the power of darkness!" (Luke 22:52–53)

As I spread lime on rutted, rocky terrain that is eighteen months away from resembling a lawn, I lament last year's unfortunate sequence of events: a builder who started too late, bad weather once he started, monsoonlike rains that washed out his first lawn seeding, his decision to finish the house but to leave landscaping undone.

Are these "bad things," in any meaningful sense of "bad"? No, just unfortunate, the sort of missed opportunity and inadequate effort that happen all the time. Besides, for my own reasons of timing, I agreed to accept an undone project.

Some things, in other words, leave us frustrated, perhaps wounded, and we need to learn from them. But are they "bad"? No, unless we are to consider any unwanted rain or bump in the road to be "bad."

What, then, is "bad"? That, it seems to me, is among our larger questions. For we live in a world of machines, electronics, well-designed systems, powerful medicines, and indoor plumbing, and such things are supposed to work smoothly and, in working, to protect us from humankind's historic sources of distress.

When they fail, we feel betrayed. Something like a power blackout or an epidemic disease isn't supposed to happen, so when it does, we look for some bad force to blame. Our concept of evil has become too broad and nebulous, which renders us both anxious about living in a world of "bad things" and paralyzed in the face of actual evil.

In the 1940s, for example, mounting evidence of the Jewish Holocaust stirred a tepid response in the United States, not because the American government was inherently anti-Semitic, but because evidence fell into a political matrix alongside other issues and was treated as a political problem, not an outbreak of evil.

The same thing happened after 9/11, when terrorism and religious extremism were treated as a political challenge and not sufficiently identified as evil.

A reader asks why bad things happen. Some things, of course, just happen. Accidents, missed flights, illnesses, sales not made, rain on parades—unfortunate, hurtful, but not bad in any meaningful sense.

Actual badness happens, too, and understanding it requires more than an awareness of suffering. Jesus seems to have understood evil as a choice, an "hour" when people choose "darkness" over light. In his instance, the religious establishment chose to ignore him when open antagonism might have exposed them to public scorn. Instead, they came after him at night, hidden from the public eye.

That cowardice and subterfuge made them tools of the "power of darkness." The same opposition, handled openly, would have caused just as much blood, but it wouldn't have made them captives of evil.

Truly bad things, it seems, arise from choices people make in fear and deceit. Even in misfortune and frailty, we are given the choice of honest or dishonest, open or hidden, accountable or evasive. Death to self and to God seems to happen when we choose deceit.

When Jesus is seen as "light," therefore, it means that Jesus names the darkness for what it is and makes the hidden known.

Allied troops, you see, eventually entered Auschwitz and gave us images that still inform our ethical systems and make us less likely to repeat that particular evil. In recent years, religious extremism has been exposed.

Darkness still occurs, for the evil one never stops trying to destroy, but every time we choose honest, open, and accountable, we help God to make the world lighter.

— Chapter 14 —

Easter

QUESTION 95: "Why won't you speak to me? For a lifetime I have prayed for guidance, for strength of will, for comfort, for some real sense of your presence, but I am answered with silence. How, then, can I have faith?"

While they were perplexed about this, suddenly two men in dazzling clothes stood beside them. The women were terrified and bowed their faces to the ground. (Luke 24:4–5)

Tonight's soccer game is great, but I tarnish it by talking too much.

I honor my vow to refrain from yelling at players, especially my son. But I do keep a sotto voce commentary going with my wife, most of it praising our kids for learning to pass and to play positions, but some of it lamenting their play.

Two comments concern forwards. One is considerably overweight and cannot keep up with the attack. I mention his need to lose weight. The other concerns a forward who is quick but won't press the attack. Our team misses several scoring opportunities because these two are lagging.

After the 2-1 loss, both players come to their parents, who happen to be sitting nearby and surely overheard my comments. I immediately regret my commentary.

Lesson: figure out which kids go with which parents. Larger lesson: be quiet.

At some point in the faith journey, this becomes the operative word: be quiet. Our worldly noise drowns out the still, small voice of God. Our personal wordiness makes no room for hearing. Even prayer can get in the way. Sometimes it is necessary just to bow our faces to the ground and let God say what needs to be said.

That is off-center behavior for believers, because our faith is primarily a matter of words. We read words, write words, gather to hear and to sing words, admire graceful words, reward effective wordsmiths in the pulpit, and, when need arises, respond with words. Our words range from the careful and intellectual to the wild and emotional. But words tend to be our bridge to each other and to God.

At some point, however, our words stand between us and God. We phrase prayers with language that soothes our spirits, but is that God's intent? We proclaim truths that make sense of what we know, but is that God's sense? We study words of Scripture, but are they God's living word?

We will never know unless we stop talking and allow a silence for God to fill. The women at the tomb were driven to that silence, first, by discovery of a missing body, and second, by the appearance of angels. They were terrified and perplexed. In response, they bowed their faces to the ground.

Then the angels could speak. Then they could explain the missing body. Then they could remind the women what Jesus had said during his ministry. Then the women had something to say.

Note that the apostles dismissed the women's words as an "idle tale" until they went to the tomb and themselves were driven to silence.

A reader asks why God won't speak to her. There is a lifetime context for her question and no simple answers. But I would commend her to silence. Not that silence which listens impatiently for an expected word, not that silence which seizes an opening to resume talking, but silence like that on Easter morning. Silence as emptiness, silence as being in the presence of something that one's own words cannot comprehend, silence as letting go of control.

Our words are ultimately about control. That's why we talk so much. Words enable us to control other people—hence the tendency of weak bosses to dominate meetings with their words, rather than listen for fresh information. Words enable us to control reality—hence our tendency to categorize, to compartmentalize, to judge, to define. Words enable us to hide and to avoid.

Faith is about letting go of control.

QUESTION 96: "Did you really arise from the dead and come back and show yourself to your disciples?"

The men said to them, "Why do you look for the living among the dead? He is not here, but has risen." (Luke 24:5)

At tonight's soccer venue, parents sit far from the field. We are distracted by conversations.

As a result, when the referee calls a foul and awards the other team a game-changing penalty kick, no one knows what happened. Parents ask each other: "What did he call? What was the foul?"

There is no instant replay, of course, so we are left to wonder and, inevitably, to fill the vacuum with our own conclusions, or not to care at all. Since it is just a game, most parents choose the not-care option. We resume our conversations.

But let's say we did care and were filling in the blanks from fleeting glimpses imperfectly remembered. An actual thing did happen. But it went by so fast. How do we respond to it? Share glimpses, of course, and maybe, cooperatively, construct a reasonable account.

But let's say one parent has an agenda: to protect or blame a child, to pursue a grudge against this referee, to create a stir, to garner attention. Now the sharing of glimpses has a new element: deliberate distortion.

In these conditions, will we ever know what happened? No, we can only deal with the consequences: another loss, deflated children, a coach trying to be upbeat, plus delayed homework and violin practice.

This is what happened on Easter morning. A few distracted women caught fleeting glimpses of something perplexing but momentous. They saw an empty tomb and heard a few words. That much seems clear. But they didn't actually see the event itself, and what they did see happened fast and was confusing.

It should be no surprise that their memories were contradictory. One angel or two? Earthquake or eerie silence? Burial cloths or not? What did the angels actually say? What were the women's names? Did Mary Magdalene stay behind or run away with the others?

Even the resurrection—one of the few consistent details in all four Gospels—was subject to the vagaries of observation and memory. To that we must add the early writers' agendas. To John, for example, the role of Mary Magdalene was critical. To Luke, Mary Magdalene was a minor detail, whereas the link to Jesus' foretelling was critical. To further his agenda of unseating the Jerusalem religious elite, Matthew inserted an account of how chief priests paid soldiers to lie.

This combination of fleeting glimpse, faulty memory, a gap of many years, and differing political agendas makes for a mess—if we needed historical accuracy. (Asserting that God "wrote" the New Testament and the contradictory details were put there by God for our edification is simply lazy biblical scholarship.) But does our faith rest on an accurate account of Easter, or of any other detail about Jesus?

A reader asks if Jesus actually rose from the dead and appeared to his disciples. Christian faith is grounded in saying Yes to both questions: Jesus did rise, and he did appear to his friends. Beyond that, however, we must acknowledge incomplete information and—a work that many Christians don't have the heart to undertake—we must sort through the church's political agendas.

The larger point, however, is that we don't look for the living God in the dead shards of history. We can make political hay from ancient details, but we can't build a faith. Like parents assessing a soccer issue, we must recognize what matters: God's ongoing life, illuminated for us in the life and resurrection of Jesus of Nazareth, and our citizenship in a godly realm where love conquers hate, joy conquers despair, goodness conquers evil, all lives are important to God, and hope appears on even the harshest days.

QUESTION 97: "I wonder if you will address a question about the need to die in order to live. What is a practical and layman's explanation for that command? It sounds very scary and always gives me pause."

[The men said,] "Remember how he told you, while he was still in Galilee, that the Son of Man must be handed over to sinners, and be crucified, and on the third day rise again." Then they remembered his words. (Luke 24:6–8)

Humility piles on humility as I work with my older sons to launch a Web site that will support and supplement my daily e-mailed meditations.

I am writing the content, but they—ages twenty-four and twenty-three—are doing the heavy lifting: programming the site's functionality, setting up security, arranging certificates, preparing "terms and conditions," and turning my efforts into pages viewable on any browser.

My job is to listen to them. They work in the field of web programming. They know how to stitch together a Website. I know where I want to end up, but it is their knowledge that will get us there.

This is a reversal, of course. It wasn't long ago that I had the knowledge and they were listening. But they are older and more experienced now. Life and hard work have given them skills different from mine.

I must abandon any illusion of parental omnipotence and listen to what they say.

A reader asks for practical guidance on dying in order to live. What did Jesus mean by that? A good question for Good Friday. A better question, in my view, than how much blood Jesus shed or how deeply the scourging cut.

On Easter morning, angels told the women two things: First, they explained the empty tomb: "He is not here, but has risen." Second, they urged the women to "remember" what Jesus had told them. Jesus had seen this coming and knew it was necessary.

This, in my view, is where the divinity of Jesus is manifest: not in supernatural powers, but in having been there before, in having been betrayed in the garden of Eden; whined against in distress; forgotten in the thrill of victory; turned into weapon, partisan, curse, and book; consulted when convenient; loved intermittently; and now rejected in the flesh.

Jesus knew, and he told his friends. It was now on them to listen. That, dear reader, is where dying to self starts. Not in being nice, loving, generous, or friendly, but in knowing one's need to listen outside ourselves. We don't know it all, cannot imagine it all, cannot study enough or invent enough or calculate enough. We know a lot, but God knows more, and the people around us know more, too.

Some of our listening hearkens backward to events recorded in Scripture and emulated in tradition. But we must listen also to life. And that is a humbling task. We must bend the knee of pride and listen to spouses, children, neighbors, and enemies. We must listen to voices that make us uncomfortable. We must allow God to call our treasured institutions and folkways into question. We must listen for the new accents, restless yearnings, and evolving presence of a living God.

As the reader says, this can be "scary." When you choose to listen, you lose control. God may be quite different from the convenient pictures we have painted. Our doctrines might be 100 percent about us, merely clever ways not to listen. Our traditions might answer questions that God never intended to ask.

Dying to self isn't like taking a course, where you know syllabus and requirements in advance. Dying to self is like falling in love, leaving home, or bearing children: you don't know where you are going, how you will get there, whom you will meet along the way, or what you will find.

It is a venture in self-emptying, not self-fulfillment.

QUESTION 98: "Lord, please help me see you more clearly."

Returning from the tomb, they told all this to the eleven and to all the rest. (Luke 24:9)

When I take a project to my favorite print shop, my account manager comes over to greet me and to confirm a special price. I thank her for being so efficient and courteous. She looks over her shoulder and says, "I want my boss to hear that."

He comes over. I repeat my praise. He is young and doesn't know what to do. So he gives her a "good girl" hug and says something mildly patronizing.

Another manager steps up. "I need to hear this, too," he says. He hands me a customer survey form. It is about the store, not the employee. He is turning praise of one employee into a career boost for himself.

It is a curious exchange. One uses surprising news to resolve a personal situation. One is awkward but genuinely pleased for a colleague. One exploits the news for personal benefit.

If that complexity greets the surprising news of one employee receiving praise, imagine the Byzantine complexity that greeted the surprising news borne by women about relocated stone, missing body, strange men telling strange news.

In Luke's version, most dismissed it as an "idle tale," not worthy of belief. Only Peter went to see for himself. In Matthew, the risen Christ greeted the women, and the men never did see the empty tomb. In Mark, the women told no one. In John, two disciples went to verify the women's news, then left. Only Mary Magdalene stayed long enough to greet the risen Christ.

The four evangelists were wrestling with a mystery: who heard the surprising news, whom did they tell, how did those hearers respond, how did the news spread?

Beneath those questions is another. If the news was so glorious, so worthy of a Handel oratorio, so momentous as to launch a worldwide institution and to change human history, why didn't it change everything right away? Why were apostles so slow to react? Why did followers of Jesus disband? Why did people of Jerusalem resume former ways?

Most perplexing to me, how did the amazing events of Easter—confusing, quiet, gentle—lead to a hierarchical, power-hungry institution with princelike prelates, rigid doctrines, self-serving certainties, brutally enforced rules, and a penchant for taking arms against all opposition?

I go back to the print shop scene. How do we handle surprising news? That, I think, is the answer to the reader's desire to see Jesus more clearly. News of God is always a surprise.

It is carried by surprising people—in this instance women, in other instances demoniacs, children, gentiles, obscure prophet, Persian king, Pharisee, foreigner, youngest son, each of them easily dismissed.

The news has surprising content. Read the stories. Read Genesis 2–3. Read Yahweh's strange dialogues with Noah and Abraham. Read the trajectory of divine mood as related by the prophets. Read the parables told by Jesus. It is all strange and chaotic.

The news leads in surprising directions. An ark for Noah, new homes, new names, unexpected childbirth, strange assignments, duels with Pharaoh and a giant, people being jerked out of sleep and family ties, old careers ending, new calls arising.

Like one print shop manager, we don't know how to handle such news, so we hug it, patronize it, reduce it to our size, and grin. Like the other, we try to manage it, turn it to our advantage. Or like the account manager, we tell someone else, but with complicated motivation.

To see Jesus more clearly, I think we need to accept surprising news, by whatever surprising voice it reaches us, and then just listen, savor, get confused, get scared, and listen more. We need to overcome our awkwardness, our desire to manage, and our reluctance just to smile and say, "Thank you."

QUESTION 99: "Tell us about Mary Magdalene, Sofia, et al., but especially Mary Magdalene. Why did you reveal yourself to her first? What was lost after Nicaea, never to be unearthed?"

Now it was Mary Magdalene, Joanna, Mary the mother of James, and the other women with them who told this to the apostles. (Luke 24:10)

All around me are signs of other days.

Coffee mug acquired in Cornwall. Globe given when my mother was healthy. Pensive photograph from a grateful parishioner. Watercolor commissioned to remember the family farm in New Hampshire. Books, artwork, and trinkets from days that made me what I am.

I also glimpse the future—projects, opportunities, dreams, challenges.

What would happen if a chunk of this treasure were cast aside? Not just lost, as mementos tend to get lost, but rejected, treated as never having happened? Not just reconsidered, in the way we revisit memories and see more in them, but erased from memory?

How could I ever know myself? How could I remain connected to my parents, and through them to my grandparents, and through them to my heritage as a citizen? How could I know the heartache, adventures, family suppers, walks, love, dreams, learning, and worrying that shaped my character and my faith? What kind of future could I build on blankness?

Such a tragedy happened in the early years of the Christian movement when women were cast aside. A few names were remembered, but the tradition-shattering way that Jesus treated women was erased, rejected, as if it never happened.

Mary of Magdala, apparently a woman of means and close friend of Jesus, was recast as a harlot. Mary the mother of Jesus, apparently a sturdy leader, was recast as a marble virgin, to be venerated in ways that would become increasingly maudlin. Women were evicted from the inner circle, shoved into an invisibility that presages the Taliban.

Jesus wasn't like that. His circle included men and women on equal footing. They traveled together, learned together, served together. Just as Jesus looked beyond artificial barriers separating Jew and Gentile, clean and unclean, so he moved beyond the historic chasm separating male and female.

We don't know why the early church reinstated that chasm. Guesses abound, some backed by scholarship, some expressed in imagining. But it seems clear that a primary thrust of Jesus' being was deliberately cast aside.

We have spent the past forty years arguing about women's roles in organized religion. We have fought over every detail, every rule, every word of liturgy, every hiring practice. We have worn ourselves out debating who gets stature. Now some fundamentalists want to turn back women's religious clocks to the 1930s and Mel Gibson trots out the legend of Mary Magdalene as harlot.

A reader asks for information about Mary Magdalene and other women. I wish we had some. Not just for reasons of justice, but because our faith is impoverished. How can we know God if an entire dimension of God's being is denied? How can we know the full meaning of creation, exodus, covenants, and promises unless we see God weeping over Jerusalem, loving in that fullness which comes when both parents love the child?

This isn't a contest to see who gets the prizes. This is about the very foundation of our faith. If we insist on God as male, disciples as male, and authority as male, we make God too small and our faith too narrow.

I remember the day Henri Nouwen told an assembly of prosperous church folk about viewing Rembrandt's *The Return of the Prodigal*. Nouwen had been broken. Now he studied a broken son kneeling before a forgiving father. The father laid hands on his shoulders.

One hand, Nouwen said, was the gnarled hand of a workingman. The other was the tapered hand of a woman.

Nouwen paused, and the audience gasped. For that, we suddenly realized, is the God before whom we all kneel.

⟣ Conclusion ⟣

QUESTION 100: "What now?"

When it was evening on that day, the first day of the week, and the doors of the house where the disciples had met were locked for fear of the Jews, Jesus came and stood among them and said, "Peace be with you." (John 20:19)

Moved by the story of Blind Bartimaeus, I invited readers of my daily meditations to send questions that they would ask of Jesus if he were passing by on the road. In all, I received nearly 400 questions, and they continue to arrive. This volume addresses 100 of them.

This has been an eye-opening and humbling experience for me. People's questions are basic, down-to-earth, making hardly any reference to doctrine, historic controversies, or ecclesiastical power struggles. Several concern church, but most concern basic life questions such as falling in love, losing loved ones, career choices, personal suffering, and societal distress, and, in the largest grouping, basic questions about faith, such as "Is it true?" and "Help me to see you."

Now that I know better what is on people's hearts—and on my own—I have less patience than ever for church arguments, doctrinal debates, dueling Scriptures, and that ugly triumphalism which insists on its own way as the only way. I find it tragic that church leaders could take all of this hunger and channel it into controversies such as sexuality or the election of bishops. If people are wondering about their marriages, jobs, and deaths, what possible use is right opinion? Do they believe that God will start or stop loving humanity because of their doctrines? How did we ever become so enamored of argument?

For too long, religion has been locked behind doors of fear. Fear of error, fear of change, fear of strangers, fear of diversity, fear of failure, fear of commitment. We instill fear in one another. Part of that is a determination to find safety for oneself by intimidating the other. Part of it is simply not knowing one another.

As an Easter people, we believe that the risen Christ comes through those doors of fear and calls us outside into lives marked by peace, servanthood, and hope. Inside, we taste the acid of argument, self-serving, and despair. Out there, we find purpose.

How will that happen? How will we see enough to find faith? Maybe through liturgy, although I suspect we have argued too much about liturgy and ordination and left little capacity to amaze. Maybe through Bible study, although Bible discussions tend to founder on "shoulds" and the unending warfare between fundamentalism and common sense. Maybe our prelates have wisdom, although I think most prelates should take a vacation from oratory and simply listen to their people.

I am coming to believe that our primary work as Christians is to know one another, to listen to the world around us, to hear the questions that greet us on arising, and in those chaotic accents and questions to witness the presence of God.

Rather than squander more time in arguing about the answers, we need to hear the questions.